THE MODERN CHANAKYA

RAHUL RAJ

Copyright © Rahul Raj
All Rights Reserved.

ISBN 979-888521885-6

This book has been published with all efforts taken to make the material error-free after the consent of the author. However, the author and the publisher do not assume and hereby disclaim any liability to any party for any loss, damage, or disruption caused by errors or omissions, whether such errors or omissions result from negligence, accident, or any other cause.

While every effort has been made to avoid any mistake or omission, this publication is being sold on the condition and understanding that neither the author nor the publishers or printers would be liable in any manner to any person by reason of any mistake or omission in this publication or for any action taken or omitted to be taken or advice rendered or accepted on the basis of this work. For any defect in printing or binding the publishers will be liable only to replace the defective copy by another copy of this work then available.

This book is dedicated to all my readers

Contents

Acknowledgements .... *vii*

1. Achieving Something Big In Life 1
2. Motivation A Myth 10
3. Procrastination 16
4. Your Happiness Is Your Responsibility Alone 21
5. Meditation 32
6. Journaling 36
7. Planning Your Next Five Years 42
8. Dopamine Detox To Do Hard Things In Life. 46
9. Right Approach Towards Relationship 51
10. Overcome Shyness 63
11. Power Of Scheduling 67
12. Power Of Emotion 71
13. Multiply Your Productivity 75
14. Gratitude 82
15. Art Of Fortune Creation 87
16. Rituals That Will Change Your Life 98
17. Mentor 107
18. Habits 112
19. Parenting 120
20. Food Habits 132
21. Boundary Setting 138
22. Critical Thinking 144
23. Mindset 159

Contents

24. Upgrading With Time	164
25. Phone And Social Media Are Killing Us	170
26. Daily Nap	176
27. Luck	180
28. Let's Talk About Porn	184
29. Sexting, Sextortion And Revenge Porn	194
30. Training Sexuality	200
31. New World Of Hyper-sexuality	209
32. Fighting The Rape Culture	219
Author	227

Acknowledgements

I owe this book to so many people who directly and indirectly supported and influence me in my journey of making this possible.

I would like to thank my parents for their love and support. I would like to acknowledge my mentor Pradeep sir for transforming my life and bringing out the best in me. It was back in class eight, I remember, when you implanted confidence in an average doing boy with almost zero faith in himself. It's because of a teacher like you that a boy who once feared sharing his opinions in a small crowd took the courage to write a book.

I thank my younger sister Kumkum for the speedy and beautiful editing. I would also like to thank my all sisters for their support especially my youngest sister Priya for helping me throughout the writing journey of this book.

I express my gratitude to all those who I met in my journey of growth for having taught me and propelled me to grow through experiences that were sometimes joyous and sometimes painful. I am grateful for them all.

A small yet important introduction

* This book is written from a perspective that what if Acharya Chanakya exists in this modern time(21st century). How would he give a solution to the problem that we face in day-to-day life?

*This book doesn't contain any translation of the writings of Acharya Chanakya. As Chanakya was a critical thinker, this book also critically analyses every thought and idea which are mainly based on your life.

* This book is a collection of ideas and perspectives of so many things. It covers some sensitive topics, so it is suitable for 13+.

*Think and reflect on the ideas you have understood.

* The best thing about this book is that you can read it from any chapter.

1

Achieving something big in life

First, you need to change the mindset of how you perceive yourself and you need to adapt to the mindset of high-performance players like Michael Jordan, Kobe Bryant, Ronaldo etc.

What do players do before their game? They train themselves before the game, they try to figure out ways to improve their performance by working on their knowledge and skills and throughout training they improve themselves. In the same way, you need to train yourself to reach your goal. You need to start your day with encouraging affirmation or self-talk. This self-talk will put you in a zone for the work and help you to be more focused and conscious. You also need to organize yourself before going to start your work like taking a bath, removing distractions from the work environment etc.

Most people tell us that they aren't able to work towards the goals they had set and this happens because they do not develop the mindset required to achieve it, they just try to do work, as a result, they are not consistent and focused. Then the question that arises is how to develop an achiever mindset – it starts with doing hard things and making sacrifices in life for long term growth. Sacrifice and obsession are needed to achieve high in life.

If you want to be great in a particular area, you have to be obsessed with it. A lot of people say they want to be great but they are not willing to make sacrifices necessary to achieve greatness – Kobe Bryant

Obsession is needed because without it you are not willing to make great sacrifices. Kobe Bryant sacrifices his friendship and love to be the top basketball player in the world, he has made sacrifices to a very extreme level. The greatest achievement you want needs you to pay for it by making a great level of sacrifice.

You need to have your spectrum of sacrifice which you are going to make for your goal depending upon what you want and up to what level.

P.V. Sindhu had not used her phone for the last three months before her main match while she was preparing for the Tokyo Olympics. Can you imagine life without social media, no internet? But she did that to stay focused on the game. She had won the silver medal and make our country feel proud.

Great achievement comes from great sacrifices.

My life, my responsibility no one is coming to save me, I need to do it of my own – Shwetabh Gangwar

Yes, you need to give up a certain amount of social life, phone, entertainment in life to reach your goal. Most people want to reach their goal without stepping out of their comfort zone and without making any sacrifices, which is not possible. Even if you can reach your goal you will not able to achieve it to the level you wanted and the period you have wished.

The second most important thing that comes for an achiever mindset is what type of information you are feeding to your brain from your phone, relationships and people around you, how your brain processes information. If you want to work at a very high level then it depends on your self-talk, which is influenced by what you're feeding your brain from the surrounding.

You need to put thoughts, people, out of your life which makes you away from your dream.

"Show me your priorities, your daily routine, books that you read, content that you consume from the internet and the person with whom you hang out the most from that I can predict your future."

The fact about a human brain is that we are not designed to do things that are uncomfortable and scary, our brains are designed to protect us from those things Our brain is trying to keep us alive.

But to make money, build a business we need to do hard things, it's our consciousness that tells us to work, make money and become successful in life.

We need to trick our brain to do uncomfortable things in life

One of the methods is explained by Mel Robbins in her book 5-second rule. The 5-second rule is simple – whenever you feel the desire to act on your goal, you must physically move within 5 seconds and start performing the work else your brain will give you thousands of reasons not to perform it and you will get into overthinking.

When you feel hesitation before doing something that you should do 5-4-3-2-1-Go and move towards action.

The counting will make you focus on your goal or commitment and distract you from worries and excuses in your mind.

I am one decision away from a different life, for my relationship, my income and my career

You need to develop a high work ethic to win in life and you also need to take ownership of your choices because distraction is not going anywhere, manage them and block them in your productive time.

Always ask yourself "what I am setting up for my future life."

How to Develop a high Work ethic?

Work ethic is a set of moral principles and values that we hold within us which guide our attitude and behaviour for the work.

These moral principles are formed by your self-beliefs, so we can say there is a direct relation between your self-belief and your work ethic. Our self-beliefs lead us to our work ethic and our work ethic leads us to our behaviour and attitude towards work and these behaviours are deciding factors whether we reach our goals or not.

Self-belief -> work-ethic-> Behaviour and attitude for work -> reach goal or not

Our work ethic is our reflection of our self-beliefs

So let's understand how these beliefs are formed and what is belief?

It is a feeling of certainty, assurance, permanence and rigidity about a thought. These beliefs are formed with the interpretation of experiences that we experience due to circumstances, people around us and tragedies which happen to us in some stages of life.

When we interpret the experiences that give us feeling (negative or positive) and from these feelings, we start making opinion and then your brain searches for proof to justify our opinion and all of this mostly happen unconsciously without your awareness and when brain get proof then these opinions transform into beliefs.

Example -: Rohit is unable to solve maths problems and from this experience, he interprets that maths is not for him and over the period, he starts getting low marks in maths.

Here, the Interpretation of Rohit that he is not for maths is his opinion about himself and when he gets low marks he gets the proof and he starts believing that maths is not for him.

Our interpretation of the situation plays a vital role. If here Rohit makes a positive interpretation that he needs to practice more maths and he will improve then over the period he can score good marks in maths. Most people are like Rohit and generally make negative interpretations of situations which leads them to destructive and wrong beliefs.

So we need to become optimistic people and try to find something good from the situations (even from bad ones) and stop being pessimistic people who will find bad things in good situations.

There are some ways by which you can sow the seed of beliefs but you need to give proof to your brain by working on it.

1) By doing positive self talk daily (Affirmation) -: Positive self-talk will build your confidence, improve attitude, helps to cope with stress, encourage motivation. Word "I am" is so much powerful. If you want to perform at peak level your conscious mind will not be enough, you need the help of your subconscious mind and affirmation is a great tool to do it. The conscious mind is the gateway to the subconscious mind. Some people become so pessimistic in life just because of negative affirmation(self-talk) they were doing over the period. Over repetition of affirmation, our brain starts to rewire and make changes in our attitude which affect our behaviour(action).

" You can't say something for very long and not have an expression of that thing manifest"

You need to emotionally feel the affirmation to make it your reality.

It's the repetition of affirmations that leads to belief and once that belief becomes a deep conviction things begin to happen –: Muhammad Ali

Story of Roger Bannister (four minutes mile)

In the modern Olympics (1954), nobody had run the mile in less than 4 minutes so all scientists, doctors, spokesperson gives the reason why you can't run a mile in less than 4 minutes. They say our lungs are not big enough if you try you will have a heart attack so everyone's self-talk (affirmation) was "I can't do it." There was a sportsperson in England named Roger Bannister

Who says "I can do it ".He does not listen to people and he keeps on doing his self-talk until one day he crashed the mile in 3:59 seconds. Form that people start changing their thinking patterns and attitude and now it can be done. In the same year, 27 runners break the 4-minute barrier and the next year 235 runners break the same 4 min barrier. This only happens because they changed their self-talk (affirmation).

Visualization -: Most Powerful way to rewire your subconscious mind, a picture is worth a thousand words. It is a recreation of the image, sounds and environment before it happens. It is a very powerful meditation used by people from ancient times to prepare the mind, body and consciousness for upcoming challenges, situations and circumstances.

Australian psychologist Alan Richardson experimented. He randomly divided basketball players into three groups

Group A:- they were instructed to practice free shots for 20 minutes for 30 days.

Group B-: they were instructed to visualise successful free shots for 20 min, but not to touch the ball.

Group C -: they refrained from basketball and visualization.

After 30 days group A improves 24%. Group B improve by 23% just one per cent less than the group that practised every day. Group C does not make improvements.

From this experiment

Visualization with emotion + practice = secret formula to get a result.

Story of Natan Sharansky -: One Russian Jews was living in communist Russia. He was accused of being an American spy, he was sent to jail. He was interested in chess from childhood so he decided to play chess with world grandmaster " Gary Kasparov" chess champion of that time. He plays chess for 12 years in his mind for 12 years.

Finally, released from jail he went to Israel where he became a cabinet minister. Gary Kasparov went to Israel to play a demonstration match (playing with five players at a time) where he defeated four of them but he lost one person.

The person with whom he lost was Natan. When Reporters asked him how he defeated the Grandmaster then Natan replied I was defeating him every day for 12 years in my mind, so I was already programmed myself to defeat him.

This story tells us how repetitive visualisation can transform thoughts into belief.

Now it's time to learn from the high work- ethic personalities -:

1) Mohammed Ali-: He believes that whatever the thing he focuses on and puts dedication, then he can learn (growth mindset). He beliefs that with a clever mind and hard work new path can be made.

2) Michael Jordan -: He says I have failed so many times that's why I am successful(learning from failure and bouncing back). He says discipline and hard work are the foundation of success. He was a competitive person and says dream big chase big.

He does not lose any opportunity to learn new and improve his game which gave him success in his career in very little time. He beliefs " Always master your basic skills".

3) Cristiano Ronaldo-: He has an elite mentality. He thinks he is among the best player in the world. So he needs to train like a champion player. He says to be Ronaldo he needs to train like it, he set high standards himself and does not feel satisfied when he does not train with his full potential.

He beliefs that there are no shortcuts.

4) Kobe Bryant-: He says be driven, most people are afraid of hard work but I am going to be the hardest worker in the room. He says that he does not get satisfied when he is not able to give 100% and feels so pain inside.

Everything is done to learn to become how to become a better basketball player, when you have this mindset, the world becomes your library to help you to become better at the craft. I got to get stronger so I got to train differently (working on improving the stronger and weaker side and balancing them).

5) Will Smith -: In his 23 years of career he was never afraid of hard work, he learned new skills and knowledge over the period. He says I can work till my last breath for my dream, there is no confusion, most people do not want to make sacrifices. He says hard work and dedication are always greater than talent. No matter how much talented you are if you are not skilled you will lose. You can go A to B from talent but to move further you need skill.

We are not trying to make a perfect wall but we are placing 1 brick in 10 minutes in the best way anyone can place it(forget about your big goal and just focus on taking small steps everyday time this will reduce the pressure of the big goal). He beliefs absolute focus is needed for world-class performance or mastery.

Neuro-linguistic programming -: To make new constructive beliefs attach good emotions(happiness, satisfaction, proud etc) to the thought that you wanted to make belief and attach bad emotions (sadness, depression, pain) to the thought that you wanted to avoid. Example-: Kobe Bryant feels so much pain when he is not able to give his 100% he had attached bad emotions for not giving 100% in the match, not training properly etc. So to avoid that physiological pain, he gives his 100% in the match.

II
Motivation a myth

We live in a world where people are obsessed with motivational content. We all pass through a period when we spend our whole day reading inspirational quotes and listening to motivational speakers where the speaker shouts, " Wake up idiot you must work like hell" and boom, we feel so excited about our goal but, that excitement does fade away the next day or the next moment. Motivation is overrated these days. Most people do not know, what motivation is or how to get it.

Motivation is an emotion that gives us a strong positive feeling to work on the desire(goals). The more they desire, the more motivated they become. Most people are confused about the source of motivation. They think that motivation is the spark that automatically produces the lasting eagerness to do hard work, the greater the motivation the more effort you are willing to put in. But actually, motivation is a result. Motivation is pride that you take in works you have already done, which fuel your willingness to do even more. It is a feeling of gratification generated by dopamine, a hormone that is triggered each time when you achieve something. Most people think that they need a motivational speaker to get them motivated towards their goal. Motivation is a word that is tossed around as a secret ingredient for success.

Let's understand the mechanism of motivational content in your brain-:

When you consume any motivational content then at that moment your brain releases chemicals like dopamine, endorphin etc which make your brain think that you are serious, focused, and you are progressing towards the goal and also give you a sense of satisfaction.

Then you go into action faking mode, where you think that you have done something and progressed. But in reality, you have not taken any action. Your brain subconsciously resister this pattern and this motivational content work as an escape from the real action.

But why do people do this?

Because people are emotional, they want to feel good and emotionally satisfied. Peoples nowadays just want to feel motivated but does not want to take action. In the short run, you can take advantage of motivational content if you are applying the pre-decide approach.

Let's say you consume motivational content for 15min and then go straight to work for the next 2hrs. But in the long run, this is not going to motivate you to achieve your big dream. We live in a world where peoples are more interested in motivational content (which give dopamine), rather than going towards solving the actual core problem that they need to address to improve.

This self-helps becomes a billion-dollar industry. There are so many people in the marketplace who gives motivation but do not address your real problems.

You need this-:

- you need clarity in your life towards your goal.
- You need a mentor (a person who has already achieved the things that you want to achieve).

A mentor does not give you fake motivation but tells you the plan, clears your path and also teaches you the skills, knowledge, mindset that you need to achieve the goal. Remember without skill you are not going to improve.

·Motivation is something that is a bi-product of action- The majority of people looking for motivation are waiting for someone to make them feel motivated, which is the wrong approach. When you take action, then your improvement/progress is what makes you feel good and that remotivates you to take more action. Actions lead to the result, and experiences from the result provide a positive emotional attachment with the result and this positive emotion brings true motivation. True motivation is powerful, long-lasting and it leads to more actions, creating a positive cycle of effortless results. No matter what you are trying to achieve if you are motivated to do it because of fear and if you are not taking the actions just because you are stressed by the size of the task in front of you so before you shrug your shoulder and spend the rest of your day watching Netflix or YouTube video, then try to take one small action to build momentum.

- **You need consistency and self-discipline-** you can't rely on emotion(motivation) to make progress towards your goal because emotion is something that sometimes comes and go. Motivation feels like waiting for doing a thing and discipline is about doing it and taking action. You need to develop self-discipline, habits to work daily, then only the result will come. Discipline is when you hold yourself to a certain standard of behaviour regardless of any change in your emotional state. You disconnect the relation between your action and your emotion – because you have told yourself you are going to do it. Our brain is designed in such a way that it consistently try to drive us away from committed action by saying things like "I will do it later", "I will do it from tomorrow" these are all tricks of our brain, as it does not want to come out of comfort zone. The funny thing about the mind is it does not stop talking and give you thousands of reasons not to do it. Making actions seem impossible until you do them. So take the first step. Take action. Take commitment and start valuing action, figure out what you want from your life (relationship, career) and take consistent action to maintain the momentum. If you want to stay motivated, if you want to stay on track, if you want to keep making progress towards the things you hope to achieve, the key is to enjoy minor victories but consistently. Consistently experiencing a genuine sense of accomplishment is what's motivate us – doing what you set to do and feeling good about it. Success is a process.

It has less to do with hoping, praying but more to do with doing the right things to move forward. Successful people feel good about themselves because they have accomplished what they set out to do today, and that sense of accomplishment gives them enough motivation they need to do when tomorrow comes.

You will stay motivated when you find a process (routine) you trust and commit to working that process for as little as a week. The power of routine is so important. When you create a routine, embrace that routine, and see the result of that routine, you will stop negotiating with yourself. Everyone has goals, but the people who achieve their goals create a routine. They build a system, they consistently take steps that ensure they reach their goal.

" If you need inspiring words don't do it"- Elon musk

How to stay focused and achieve your goal without relying on external motivation?

The problem with our brain is that we mostly forget that –"why you have started working on your specific goal and also you forget or does not have clarity about what you will get after achieving it. Due to this your brain starts focusing on the labour, or we can say efforts which are required to achieve it, as a result, you feel a lack of motivation towards your goal and start procrastinating. So you must constantly remind yourself that why you have started all this and what you will get after achieving your goal. These two things your " why" and " result" will going to empower you to keep working towards your goal.

To have clarity -: Take a journal and write " why you have started all this", " why you have chosen this goal", " what you are going to get at the end from it".

Another reason which causes a lack of motivation towards your goal is that " you have chosen an unworthy goal", most of the time we just choose our goal based on external motivation and influence to get social validation, greed for power and money etc. As a result, you never feel connected, committed and dedicated towards your goal as you have just chosen based on external influence due to this you lose the drive to achieve it and lastly, you find that you got distracted.

The real inspiration should come from within for your goal, don't be a part of the rat race and choose your goal carefully.

Ask this basic question –

- " How and why I have chosen this goal"
- "is this goal is my own or coming from external influence.

• What is the result of all this,

We usually don't address these basic questions, as a result, we keep struggling with a lack of motivation.

"Distractions are not powerful your goal is powerless" – Acharya Prashant (author)

Choose a goal that gives you joy and pleasure while working on it, even if there is no further reward is present at the end.

" Laziness comes when you're chasing money instead of the game where you love the process"- Gary Vaynerchuk

III

Procrastination

Almost everyone procrastinates sometimes and puts some of their work off. But it becomes a problem when you become a chronic procrastinator and frequently puts things off or delays the work.

Waiting is a trap, there will always be a reason to wait- **"the truth is there are only two things in life reasons and results, and reason simply does not count."- Robert Anthony**

Over the period, you will feel stressed, frustrated, self hate towards yourself for not working towards your goal. Procrastination is something that most of us have experienced. No matter how much committed and organized we are, it is difficult to fight against it.80%-95% of college students are engaged in it, 15%-20% of general people are chronic procrastinators. 95% of procrastinator wants a genuine solution and reduce it as it's hindering their professional growth in some way.

How procrastination happens – why do we procrastinate? What going on in our brain that causes us to avoid or delay the task? our brain works on the pain and pleasure principle. It always wants to escape from pain and gravitate toward pleasure. To get pleasure, your brain runs towards instant gratification (short term pleasure or pleasure in a moment). Let's call this part of the brain - monkey brain. It does not care about your future nor it has any memory of the past, it just focuses on the fun at the moment. As time passes, your rational brain makes you aware that you have not done work and as a result, you feel guilt, self-hate and other bad emotion. When you come near the deadline date of your work then, your rational brain feels pressure and fear, as a result, the rational brain takes control over the monkey brain. Let's understand it by imagining two selves-:

- Present self
- Future self

When you set long term goals for yourself E.g.- losing weight, learning a new skill, you envision what you want your future to look like. Future self-value long term rewards but only the present self have the power to take the actions required to reach your future goals. But there is a problem with the present self, it adores and loves instant gratification. As a result, we procrastinate. Future self wants to be slim and fit but present self wants cakes and sweets.

How to overcome procrastination -:

1. Break down your goals into small actionable work-: you need to first have a clarity of your goals, what you want to achieve then divide your goals into small actionable and measurable goals.

Example-: Suppose your goal is to read a 250-page book in a week, then your micro goals will be to read 36 pages every day, this micro goal is actionable and measurable. Your micro goals should fit in your daily schedule. If you are writing a book, instead of measuring your progress based on the completion of a chapter, try to measure it by – writing 3 pages in 3 hrs.

The reason we procrastinate is that our brain wants to seek immediate rewards for doing any task. If you can find a healthy reward that would be helpful for you, give small rewards for acting immediately on your task and give punishment immediately for avoiding or delaying the task. But you should train yourself for delayed gratification if you want to live a successful life.2. Apply the Pomodoro method-: Convince yourself to work for just 20min or even less on your goals because our action and behaviour are ruled by momentum. When you gain momentum or come into a flow state than because of your action you get the motivation to work more.

"Action comes first motivation follows "

When you work towards your goal consistently every day even just for one hour, you maintain your momentum. You can apply the fifteen-minute rule which states –" when you start doing any new task, tell your mind that you are going to do it for just fifteen minutes." The idea is to make your task easy as possible to get started and then momentum will carry it. If your task is easy to start, then you will less likely to procrastinate.

3. Remove distraction from work environment-: Your impulses will be high if you work in the distracting environment. So take care of your internet, notification and people around you. Having a fixed workplace will condition your brain to be interested and work with focus.

Also ask one question from yourself that "Are you trying to escape from reality and using your phone to pass the time" if the answer is yes, try to know why?

4. Give timeline -: when you give a timeline for your goal then your brain comes under pressure to complete the task. Research has shown that a long deadline or having no deadline at all lead peoples to procrastinate on a task or not complete it at all. People having shorter deadlines are more likely to accomplish the task and are less likely to procrastinate.

5. Average of five people-: If you hang out with low performers, your subconscious mind will rewire to be less productive and you will have less desire to work. If your friends are procrastinators then, most likely you will also do the same.

6. Simple rule -: Prioritise AND execute

If you are overthinking about the work & procrastinating. Apply simple rules of making a priority and execute. Make a checklist of tasks to be done according to priority and simply start executing them immediately. Rocket scientists use this method to execute complex tasks & make them simple. It will be a visual cue to trigger your behaviour or habit and measure your progress. A visual cue is something that you can see and encourage you to take action. Visual cue reminds you to start behaviour and help you to track your progress. Everyone knows consistency is essential for success, but very few people measure their progress. Visual cues exaggerate your motivation to work, the more visual progress you can see the more motivated you will be to finish the task.

7. Idea of working better under pressure is a myth- A lot of times we hear from someone that they work better and are productive under pressure. If you think it does then you are deluding yourself in a way that could be destructive. Tim pychyl, a psychologist and director of a procrastination research group, tell us that there is not one study that supports that people perform better under the gun of a fast-approaching deadline. Yes, the deadline is important as it creates work pressure, but if you have a mindset that you will perform well under pressure is wrong. You will get into stress and your ability to learn and think creatively will suffer. If you believe that you will always perform well under pressure then you will always delay your work till the last moment and never be able to leave your procrastinating behaviour.

Another major reason most people procrastinate is that they make a goal by the influence of other people, as a result, they lose motivation because the goal that they have chosen does not come from inside of them, they were externally motivated. You need to be intrinsically motivated for your goals. The majority of peoples are just focusing on the result and does not enjoy the process of getting there.

When you start enjoying the process you will never procrastinate.

IV
Your happiness is your responsibility alone

We all want to be happy, but many of us don't know how to get happiness in life. Many of us believe that the ultimate aim of our life is to be happy which might be true to a great extent. To find happiness in life, we try so many things by seeing others what makes them happy and we copy things from others so that we can get happiness but many of us fail to get it. Happiness is a very broad term in itself and its definition varies from person to person.

Maybe for some people having a lot of money makes them happy, for someone having a good life partner, for someone it could be getting fame, for a student it could be getting good marks to make him happy, for a monk it could be living a spiritual life etc.

From this, we can understand that our mindset and perception to see things play a vital role in our happiness.

The Greek philosopher Aristotle divided happiness into two parts -: Hedonia(happiness from pleasure) and Eudaimonia (happiness from the purpose).

We can simply divide happiness into two categories -:

• Short term happiness(comes by doing pleasure activities) -: Happiness that you get instantly but its effect fade away in a very short time. Even if you try to extend it you will not be able to do it.

Example-: Playing video games, drinking alcohol and taking drugs, having sex, talking with girlfriend/ boyfriend, watching funny videos, scrolling social media apps, reading memes etc. All these activities give us short term happiness and are driven by doing activities that give us pleasure.

• Long term happiness-: It is a state of mind where you feel satisfaction, joy, contentment, serenity and fulfilment which give you positive emotions. Its effect stays for a long period and this is the happiness most of us want in life.

This type of happiness comes by making some contribution to this world, having stability in life, making some good decisions in life according to your own will and not by the influence of other people. It comes by being aware of kindness and humanity. Long-term happiness is a very broad term and there are so many ways to get it, but mainly it has two components:-

Positive emotions – We all experience both negative(anger, pain, grief) and positive emotions(joy, feeling of love, radiance) in our life. But happiness is about experiencing and being in a state of mind where you feel more positive emotions than negative in a major portion of your life. Overall life satisfaction – your happiness also depend greatly upon how much you are satisfied with your work, career, relationship, achievement, family and other important things in your life. In this chapter, you are mainly going to focus on long-term happiness.

You might be thinking of yourself and have been confused about happiness. To know whether you are happy or not you need to first ask these questions to yourself and try to truly answer them.

1) Are you living the life that you wanted to live, Are you doing the work that you always wanted to do, how is your relationship, did you accomplish or will able to accomplish things that you want to do, how do all of these things mentioned above make you feel?

2) How satisfied you are with your life?

3) How do you feel about the condition of your life? Is it good or bad?

4) Which (positive or negative)emotion do you feel more if you see your overall life? One important that you need to understand is that happy people also feel a whole range of emotions – anger, joy, frustration, grief, loneliness, sadness in life but even when they face tragedy/difficulties they have an underlying sense of optimism that things will be going to better soon.

The core of long term happiness -: The starting point of long-term happiness is to listen to your " deep inner voice" what do you want and what makes your inner self happy. The majority of us never actually listen to our deep inner voice and try to copy the world. From the world, we get the wrong idea of happiness because most people are confused about long term happiness and due to this people think that – looking cool, dominating other people, building muscle, earning a lot of money, getting sexy life partners etc will make them happy.

Majority of these activities you do because of acceptance, attention, approval and appreciation which can only make you happy in the short run. But for long-term happiness

You need to first question yourself " what is the thing that makes my deep inner self happy, forget about the world" what are the small activities that make you happy. Majority of us never actually listen to our deep inner voice and try to copy the world. From the world, we get the wrong idea of happiness because most people are confused about long term happiness and due to this people think that – looking cool, dominating other people, building muscle, earning a lot of money, getting sexy life partners etc will make them happy. Majority of these activities you do because of acceptance, attention, approval and appreciation which can only make you happy in the short run. But for long-term happiness

You need to first question yourself " what is the thing that makes my deep inner self happy, forget about the world" what are the small activities that make you happy.

Remember you will never be happy in the long term if you ignore your deep inner self voice.

How to seek long term happiness

1) Develop self-discipline -: You might be thinking that self-discipline and happiness are two different things and there is no relation between them, but that is not the truth. There is a direct connection between them. First, when you listen to your deep inner self voice, you will be able to find out what you want to achieve and pursue in life which will make you happy. But if you are not self-disciplined you will never be able to accomplish the goals that you always wanted to do. We all have some behaviour which we know are not good for us and if not be fixed it will affect our lives negatively and here self-discipline plays a vital role to fix them and manage in such a way that does not hinder your goals. You need to have a set of rules to live a happy life, you need to ask your deeper self what are things that are acceptable and not acceptable.

What are the things that are acceptable from people, you need to have a boundary in your relationship and also for your wrong behaviour/ habits. You need to go deep into self-talk to find out what are your habits that are needed to be changed. When you live life with your own set of principles and set boundaries then, your self-esteem starts rising.

You will feel that you are not the person anymore that used to waste time on the phone, with wrong people, sitting lazily not doing anything, this will boost your self-esteem and give you an inner sense of satisfaction and happiness. You will feel that you are in control of yourself. Self-discipline will create a stable foundation for your life.

2) Pursue your intrinsic goals-: The problem with most of us is that most of our goals are formed due to extrinsic motivation. You copy the world so that you can get attention, appreciation and validation from people around you.

You never sit down and spend time with yourself that what are the things you want to accomplish or to do that you need to forget about the world.

You never pursue and form goals based on intrinsic motivation. Most of your goals are either externally motivated or formed by someone else (mostly parents). For example- maybe you always wanted to do some creative work but because of extrinsic motivation and validation you are working in a software firm(living unmotivated and frustrated life). You will never be happy if you always ignore the voice of your deeper inner self.

What you can do -: Pursue intrinsic goals, find out what you want to do which will make you happy, forget about the world. What type of relationship and partner you want – go deeper into question, what should be their characteristic it might be kindness, intelligence, well- educated, emotionally and financially stable etc.

3) Work on your relationships -: Our social support(friends and family) plays a significant role in our well being. One of the studies found that 43% of our happiness depends upon social supports. Quality matter more than quantity, having fewer close/supportive/ trusted friends and family members has a great impact on our overall happiness compared to having a lot of casual friends. Spend time with your friends and family and work on forming a meaningful relationship rather than wasting your time on screens. Prioritize your relationships because your loved ones will be by your side in the ups and downs of your life.

4) Reformulate your negative thoughts-: people have a natural tendency to focus more on the negative things compared to focusing on positive things. Most of us are negatively biased and have a default mindset of thinking negatively. In our mind, we exaggerate things even when the problem is small but in our mind, we made it big. Reformulating your negative thought does not mean you will ignore the negative things but it means you will become more realistic while approaching the problem.

5) Find great purpose in your life-: Purpose means seeing your life having a goal, direction and meaning. Research has found that people who feel that they have purpose have higher life satisfaction. How to find a sense of purpose -:

• Explore your area of interest – Try different things, read different types of books, learn new skills, work on your hobbies.

• Working against injustice

- Engaging in prosocial activities(an action that is a concern for the welfare of others).

Contributing values to society without any greed of return of anything. Live your life for a big purpose and have a goal that will not only be limited to yourself but also going to positively impact others. Have a goal that brings a new revolution to society. Maybe you wanted to open a school, hospital, wanted to provide education to poor people etc. Live your life for these types of purposes.

Stop valuing the wrong things-: We overvalue things like social status, money, power etc, as a result, we choose the wrong careers and goals in our life just because of external motivation. Many people think that the more money they will have the happier they will be, but that does not happen.

New research found that money does not buy happiness after $90,000 of annual salary, earning more than that annually does not have any effect on your emotional well being. I am not telling you not to earn a good amount of money and social status but I am telling you not to be so much attached to a great extent that it starts affecting your emotional well being. Pursue goals that result in enjoyment and more free time, spend your money on buying real-life experiences (travelling) rather than spending it on the material possession, you will be much happier.

6) work on your past trauma(working on mental health) -: In our life we all have to go through ups and downs, it could happen at any stage of our life. So we need to manage our stress, frustration and other negative emotions so that we can live a happy life. Especially in our country where the majority of the population comes under the middle-class family, where there is some type of struggle in day to day life. There is a great need to have an understanding and knowledge about mental health for managing stress, frustration, anger and negative emotions. Stress in our life could be caused by any difficult situation like – when there is a great loss in business, maybe even after putting a lot of effort and dedication you are not able to qualify for the exam, you have a breakup, maybe a girl rejected you, someone close dies etc. We all humans have certain limits to take the pressure(stress) but, when the limits get crossed then it results in depression and consistent sadness in life, you should always try that this should not happen to you. Stress and pressure is not always a bad thing it helps us to accomplish big things in life, and without them, you will get into a comfort zone and do not be able to accomplish great things in life. As an iron rod have to go with so much stress to become a sword, similarly you have to also go with a certain amount of stress and pressure which will shape your character and personality which is further needed to achieve great things in life. So there is a need for a balance of pressure(stress) in our life.

If there is so much pressure and stress accumulated inside of you, what do you think, what needs to do? The answer is to release pressure and stress and other negative emotions from you. You need to release it with the help of mainly emotional expression and sometimes with the help of physical expression. You need to express your deep inner feeling rather than suppress them inside of you.

The method which will help you to release stress and frustration from you-:

1) Share it with someone -: Tell your thoughts or express your emotions to someone whom you trust in life. It could be your parents, siblings, friends, spouse etc. While sharing if you are flooded with emotion let it come out, it's okay to cry, shout, abuse while sharing your problems or traumatic event. Maybe you will get solutions for your problem and even if you don't you will feel so much light from inside. Now, if you don't want to share with your close one, share your thoughts with strangers on the online platform, you can also share your problem anonymously if you want to. Strangers can understand your problem and can give you better solutions as they are not biased to traumatic events/ causes of stress.

2) Try expressive journaling -: If you don't want to share your thoughts with anyone then try expressive writing. Take a journal and start with about - the past incident of trauma, try to express your emotions as much as possible, you can use sad music to stimulate your emotions(remember while writing it's okay to cry). Do this practice for consistency 3-4 days and at last, you can burn the papers and let it go.

3) Practice physical expression -: Go to the alone place and shout, it will help you to relieve pressure and stress from you. Engage in physical activity – start doing exercise, if possible go and hit the gym, go for running, play games like football, basketball etc, join clubs to learn martial arts and at last dance and join clubs of dance.

4) You need to cry-: Crying is so much important, you need to cry by remembering that traumatic event/ incident that has happened in your life. You can listen to sad music or any music which trigger your emotion and remember that incident (use the headphone or load music) so that your suppressed emotions could come out.

But the problem with most people (especially men and some women) thinks that crying is a sign of weakness, but there is a great need to change this type of thinking and mindset. And crying should be normalized in our society both for men and women. Especially the problem with most men is that they think that it's not manly to cry as a result they usually bottle up their emotions and try to hold so many emotions(sadness) inside of them which further causes depression. If you look at the data on depression you will find that men are two times more likely to get depression compared to women. The main reason is that society always portrayed men as tough and see crying as a weak trait that every man should avoid. Parenting is also a factor where boys were taught not to cry. We all have heard things like

" Be a man don't cry"

In reality, these all are bullshit concepts created by society. Due to all these things – most men do not know how to process their emotions. Also bottling up emotions inside creates so much frustration and further lead to violent behaviours.

If you analyse the data of violent and psychopathic men criminals you will find that most of them have so much frustration inside them, which happens just because they do not know how to process emotions. Bottling up emotions and suppressing emotions not only causes mental health problems but also physical health problems causing many chronic diseases – like heart strokes, cancer, Alzheimer, cardiovascular disease etc. In India, heart strokes are common because many men do not know how to deal with stress and frustration and to process negative emotions healthily.

There is a great need to normalize crying for both men and women.

A short poem dedicated to all men especially for those who have gone or going through thought time -:

"Men Do Cry"
In the darkness of night
His dreams fight

Cause of expectations he dies
And the society always lie
" They say men don't cry"
He shouts, He sobs, He cries tight
To make his heart and mind feel light
And this all happens in the silence of night
But they say " Men don't cry"
His dreams, his wishes and his goals buried
He tells his parents not to be worried
And again in the morning he smiles
Letting his thoughts got lost for a while
But they will say " Men don't cry"
Loving someone by his whole heart
And getting drifted apart
Sometimes because of the society
And sometimes because of the lover
This all destroy him inside
Felling hurt like hell
He cries until his eyes swell
Will they still say that men don't cry
And if yes then will you tell me why?
-: Unknown

V

Meditation

Most people nowadays become conscious of their physical health, as there are parameters such as body weight, cholesterol levels, blood pressure etc, by which we can judge whether the person is healthy or not. But most people ignore their mental health as we do not have any visible parameter by which we can say a person's mental health is good or bad. We go to do workouts in the gym, running and other physical activities to maintain good physical health but most of us are not aware that our mind is a muscle and it also needs exercise. The most common and effective exercise for our brain is " mediation".

We need to recognize the fact that we have evolved technologically and things got easier but most of us have detached from nature as a result - stress, depression, other mental health issues becoming common. Mediation is an exercise for our brain to maintain peace of mind, become focused, boost happiness, enhance concentration, give clarity about what you want and things that you don't want, it enhances your consciousness. We live in a world that is full of distractions like social media constantly rewire our mind for instant gratification and reduces our focus and concentration power, provides stress but to succeed or achieve something big we need to be focused person and mediation train our brain for it. We all know that in our life we all face ups and downs, someday we celebrate and someday we get demotivated and feel like quitting or might face failure, mediation helps us to deal with stressful situations in our lives in a better way.

Mediation sets you in a state of calmness and higher consciousness and opens the path for spirituality.

Few benefits of meditation

• Stress reduction-: It decreases stress and anxiety by lowering the production of cortisol and adrenaline in our body which creates a state of deep relaxation in which our blood pressure decreases and we start taking a short deep breath.

• Improve mood-: It increases dopamine and serotonin levels by stimulating regions of our brain associated with happiness.

• Improve brain function-: It increases whole-brain function by synchronizing the right and left hemispheres of the brain by increasing Alpha, Delta and theta waves.

• Slow down ageing process-: New research has found that meditations in the long term increase grey matter, cortisol thickness and hippocampus which improves our learning abilities, memory power and decision-making ability.

Stress is one of the main reasons for premature ageing. Practising meditation promotes cell longevity and decreases stress hormones.

• Improves sleep quality by stimulating high melatonin levels.

How to meditate

First find a comfortable place where you can sit without distraction for at least 10-15 minutes, sit comfortably with your backbone straight without any back support if possible. Close your eyes and start taking deep breaths at least 10-12 times, it will set you in a relaxing and calm state. Now start focusing on your breath, feel your inhale and exhale air, if you notice that your mind starts thinking something else then return your focus to your breathing. This is simple and effective mindfulness meditation. If you don't want to focus on breathing then visualize or affirm. You can also show gratitude by bringing in mind 5-10 things that you are grateful for. This will fill you with positivity and happiness. Practice forgiveness-: bring your focus to anyone with whom you had a conflict, imagine that person in front of you, apologize for any wrong you had brought to them, ask for their forgiveness.

Forgive them if they had brought something wrong to you. Visualize yourself living your dream life, try to feel the emotions. You can also play calm, relaxing music in the background and focus on it.

There are some miss concepts regarding mediation-:

1. It is related to specific religion -: This is a common widely spread myth that meditation is a religious practice. Anyone from any religion can practice it. If we attach and restrict to a specific religion then that would be bullshit.

Yes, religious gurus perform meditation because it opens the door for spirituality but we should not forget its other benefits. Yes, you can avoid chanting and replace it with different styles of meditation. So, Change your mindset that it's only practised by gurus and see it as a brain exercise.

2. I can't meditate because my mind is always busy thinking-: Reality is that it's difficult to control your mind but it's not impossible. When you sit to do meditation focusing on breathing, chanting or visualizing then your mind will start thinking of random things / random thoughts come to your mind but your main aim should be to get back to your initial focus state.

Over the period by focusing and concentrating on one thing your brain gets rewired and makes you a more focused person.

3. I don't have time-: you don't need to dedicate so much time, just give 10-15 minutes in it. Don't make excuses. Everyone has 24 hr only, it's all about priority. Make this mindfulness technique a priority, you will be amazed by its results.

VI
Journaling

Journaling is one of the best ways to track and reach your goal (health, spiritual, financial, relationship etc). If you learn the art of asking the right questions, then you will master critical thinking skills in very little time. Almost everyone has some goals in their life but not everyone can reach them, but if you are tracking your goals then there is a major chance that you will be able to achieve them in the decided time frame. When you write your goals in a paper, in that moment miracles start to happen but even knowing that fact, most people are not able to use this powerful weapon because they see it as a waste of time. They think what's the difference between having a vision on their mind and in papers.

Writing has so many benefits. When you write you can express your thoughts in the paper, as a result, it helps you to get mental clarity. Most people search for motivation to perform the task but in reality, they are not able to do the task and procrastinate because they lack clarity.

There are so many reasons and benefits to writing a journal

1) Writing therapy heals trauma -: As we all know that life doesn't go in a smooth flow, we have to go through ups and downs in life. Sometimes in down moments of our life such as the death of loved ones, breakup, rejection etc. All these emotions sometimes are not able to completely come out from us and we continue to be in a traumatic state. Journaling is one of the best ways to heal yourself from any type of trauma you have faced. The best advantage of writing therapy is that it is accessible, portable, affordable and creates self-awareness and self-understanding. To get benefit from this therapy people should find meaning in traumatic memory and allow themselves to feel all the associated emotions with it, they should not try to suppress their bad emotions inside them and should cry if they want to. Writing about your feelings will make you less intense which directly improves your emotional health.

By doing this exercise, the person will feel significant stress reduction, it helps you to get a new perspective to see it. If you do this exercise 3-4 times for the same traumatic event then you will be able to get lessons from it (if possible) and also set yourself free from suffering.

There is no rule for expressive writing, you just need to express as much as possible. The best thing about this type of writing is that you can maintain privacy and it allows you to heal silently, without telling the world about your traumatic event.

No judgment no pressure, you can go over events in life that you don't want to disclose to anyone.

HIV patients who wrote about negative life experiences produce higher CD4 lymphocyte counts, a cell that helps restore balance in the immune system. In another study, subjects who wrote about traumatic experiences before receiving the hepatitis B vaccine had a stronger immune response allowing them to produce more antibodies.

2) Journaling enhance more chances to reach your goals -: when you write your goal and makes a plan to achieve then you will be able to think more critically and able to find answers to most of the questions and also able to see your goal with a new perspective which is going to help you. Most of the time people make plans in their heads and over the period, their thoughts fade away, as a result, they are not able to get clarity about their goals. But when you write your goals and make practical plans to achieve them, then you can easily measure your progress.

Also, it helps you to break your goals into small actionable tasks which ultimately reduce the pressure that you get when you see your big goal and also reduce the chance of procrastination, as you just need to take a small action.

Many people just randomly take action, as a result, they are not able to reach their goals in time.

Daily journaling for tracking your goals and habits is going to help you in achieving your goals. When your brain sees that you are consistently progressing towards the goal then it boosts your self-esteem and fills you with motivation to do more work.

3) Journaling improves our thinking capabilities -: writing down our ideas and thoughts help us to think more deeply and to explore boundaries. If you learned the significance of asking the right question while writing then you will automatically learn how to think critically. Most of the time our thoughts are manipulated and biased but, when we write them down we can easily deconstruct the situation and able to reach the solution.

You can ask these simple questions like-:

- What are the situation and people who drain your energy and what are the things that boost your energy and enthusiasm?
- What I can learn from this situation and this person?
- What are the choices and habits I require to reach my financial and fitness goals?
- What are the values and standards you have for your relationship and what qualities do you want in your partner?
- What should my life look like in the next 2 years? What are the things I need to accomplish to live my dream life?
- You can analyse your behaviours and decision from another point of view or perfection, it will help you to understand how to deal with challenges in life.
- You can reflect on the things that make you behave in a certain way.
- What are the things that matter in my life?
- Why do I chase toxic relationships? It will help you to know how your childhood trauma affects your present life.
- What are the ways by which you can heal yourself from past trauma?
- How you can balance your work life and family life?

In this way you can ask so many questions, this will help you to understand yourself and also help you in making decisions.

" Words are a lens to focus one' s mind" -: Ayn Rand

4) Journaling helps us to document memories -: yes, we all had gone through some past experiences that we never want to forget.

These happy memories are very close to your heart.

Nowadays photos and videos have taken the place of documenting memories, even then when you write about any event in your own words, you will feel more connected to it. Writing about positive experiences will boost our mood and remove self-doubt. Happiness coach Shawn Achor revealed that when people wrote three good things about themselves for 21 days, it led to the release of endorphins(happiness hormone) in their brain, which makes them happier and optimistic.

5) Journaling improves sleep quality -: Most people go to bed at night with worries, as a result, they are not able to get quality sleep. But when you practice journaling for just 10 minutes before going to bed then you will find that you are in a calm state, one of the best things you can do before going to bed at night is to practice a gratitude journal.

This will help you to be more optimistic and raise your happiness index. Also, we have submerged so much in technology, so journaling can be one of the best ways or rituals to disconnect yourself from your smartphone. The more you use your phone near bedtime, your mind will be filled with garbage thoughts.

Types of journaling

• Bullet journal -: It is one of the most effective and simple ways to track your goals.

" The bullet journal is an analogue system designed to track the past, organise the present and plan for the future"- Ryder Carroll (inventor of bullet journal)

How to make a bullet journal – The first page of your journal should be the index. Make a list of all habits and goals you are going to track.

These include -:

a) Self–care -: Reading, going to bed on time, spending time alone, skincare routine, spending less time on social media time, listening to music etc.

b) Health-: Daily work out, tracking water consumption, mediation, no sugar, no coffee, no smoking, tracking alcohol consumption etc.

c) Finances -: Budget, saving, tracking investment in real estate, gold, stock.

d) Relationship-: spending quality time with a family, random act of kindness, playing with kids/ pets.

Make a checklist/ To-do list or any other tracking system for your goals.

• **Gratitude journal** -: This type of journaling is best to gain optimistic views in life, also this will help you to appreciate what you already have in your life.

This type of journaling is recommended for everyone especially for those who are going through depression or a tough time in their life.

• **Self-reflection journal** -: You can ask yourself how you feel about a certain situation, people or place, How much you have grown up from last year, why you behave in a certain way around some people, how you handle stress in your life.

Is there any better way you can deal? There are so many questions you can ask which help you to be yourself.

• **For gathering knowledge** -: yes, we all get new information's every day, we read books, attend seminars, webinars etc, but over the period we forget about the knowledge we previously got.

But when you journal and make a summary after reading a book, attending seminars then you can easily retain information for a longer period.

Sometimes when we are having conversations with people, they tell their stories and experience. These stories of someone's life can teach you many lessons.

Life is short to learn from just your own mistakes, to achieve highness you must learn a lesson from someone's experience of success and failure.

VII

planning your next five years

Having a vision allows you to get clarity about your future and what you want to get out of it – whether that's a month, a year or five years. We all have different dreams for our future, getting clear about your vision will help you to create a life that is most fulfilling to you. Creating a vision for your future act as a roadmap that will guide your daily choices and ensure that your actions are aligned with your goals.

" If you are working on something exciting that you care about. You don't have to be pushed, The vision pulls you."- Steve jobs

Imagine and construct your long-term vision in a way that excites you. One of the most important traits of successful people is that they think in the long term. You can't reach your destination if you do not know where you are going. Successful people think a long way into the future and they adjust their behaviours to assure that they will achieve their long term goals. Research has found that people who have a long-term vision and who practice delayed gratification always move up economically in the course of their lifetime. When you spend weeks, months and years developing your skill, knowledge and ability to expand your experiences to be successful, you have a long term vision. They have a clear vision of what they want, which drives them to achieve it. Successful people's become prosperous because they are so much clear about what they want in the coming 5 years or even 10 years. According to which they make choices and plan to accomplish their goals.

Now it's your time to plan what you want in the upcoming 5 years. Write down your ideal life in the upcoming 5 years and also write what are the choices and habits you are going to make to accomplish them. You are more likely to achieve your goals when you write them down. Use the power of writing down your goal if you want to achieve them. Writing down your goals helps you to create a vision in your mind about your dream ideal life. The more clear you are about your desire, the more driven you will become. Clarity brings drive.

The reason why you should have written goals

1. It creates a concrete form of your dream-: writing down your goals make it tangible which helps you to interact with it. When you write it, you have described it, you give a deadline to yourself.

2. Writing down goals helps you to use the maximum potential of your brain-: when you desire and dream of something in that particular time, you use your right side of your brain which govern imagination and when you write down your goals and start actively thinking about it, describing it, then you begin to use the left side of your brain which governs your logic.

When both sides of the brain work and focus on one desire that's when a miracle starts to happen.

3. Writing them down concentrate your efforts -: when you write down your goals then your intention gets more focused on achieving that goal. And we all know the importance of focus to achieve something. The more laser-focused you are, the more concentrated your efforts will be to achieve it.

4. Make you 42% more likely to achieve them-: studies have found that writing a goal makes it 42% more possible to achieve them compared to the person who doesn't write it.

5. Increase your motivation-: when you write your goals down on paper then you are subconsciously giving yourself a command to pursue it and if anytime you get distracted, then your subconscious mind reminds it and create stress for not doing it.

As a result, you get back on track. It creates a system of self-accountability in your life.

In this similar way, you need to make a plan for -:

- Your Relationship and family
- Your personal growth
- Your adventure, fun and travel
- Your contribution to society, environment, humanity.

It can be very useful to deeply imagine a future which you would like to avoid. You probably know people who have made a bad decision in their life and end up with a life that no one wants.

Now spend some time thinking, what your life would be if you fail to pursue your goals if you let your bad habits govern your life which ends up your life full of suffering and bitterness. Imagine your life in the next 5 years if you fail to stay on the path, you need to also be clear about how you are going to manage the use of drugs and alcohol, toxic people around you etc as these things can easily distract you from the path you had chosen. Use your imagination to draw knowledge about the pain and anxiety you will feel when you will not be able to live the life you wanted to. Doing this makes you clear about what you want and things that you don't want, so that you can run away from the things that you don't want and run towards the things that you do want. Lastly, implement your idea by making monthly and weekly plans. Also, write down the worst future that you don't want – Let's say you are trapped in drug and alcohol abuse, spending your time with toxic people and getting the wrong mindset, getting bad habits and then see how does your life look like.

VIII
Dopamine detox to do hard things in life.

Our brain always wants to be happy, so it tries to do things that give pleasure. Dopamine is a neurotransmitter produced in our brain which acts as a chemical messenger, it releases when you do activities that are rewarding and pleasurable.

There is so much misconception present on the minds of many people that it's an addictive brain chemical, but in reality, it's important to have a healthy balance of dopamine as it facilitates our motivation, energy level, focus. Low dopamine results in depression, lack of motivation and concentration, memory issues, low sex drive etc. But so much high production result in addiction to drugs, alcohol, porn, excessive eating etc.

Serious health issues can develop. Dopamine motivates you to take action towards your goals and gives you a surge of reinforcing pleasure when you achieve them. Things like phones, social media, movies, YouTube, music, sex, porn, fast food give our brain a large amount of dopamine, as a result, our brain always wants to perform these tasks.

While, things like exercise, reading books, writing, coding etc releases less amount of dopamine.

We need to understand that our brain is designed in such a way that it always seeks pleasure and rewards. Our smart brain tries to get maximum rewards by putting less effort as possible, as a result, it is really on instant gratification. But the problem arises when we use social media, movies, eat fast foods then these activities increase our dopamine level so high from its normal level and after that when we try to perform tasks like studying, writing, exercise, then it produces less dopamine, as a result, we get less pleasure and feel uninterested and less motivated. Procrastination, self-doubt, lack of enthusiasm are linked with low levels of dopamine.

Again we go to do a task that produces high dopamine. Even after performing high dopamine activities, over a period our brain get used to it and crave more of it to get the same level of satisfaction and pleasure.

Let's understand with an example -: If you eat pizza continuously for 15 days then on the first day your brain feels so much good but on the fifteenth day you do not feel the same level of satisfaction because our brain develops a tolerance for the dopamine level and wants more of it to feel pleasure.

Ways which helps you to balance dopamine-:

1. One day of dopamine fast once a weekend-: Just for one day avoid things which give you high dopamine, cut down social media, phone, sex, junk foods. This day you only focus on your thought, you can read books, plan your future life by journaling, exercising. It is not completely possible to "fast" or eliminate dopamine from your body because this hormone is released whenever you see food, your friends, even after performing moderate body movement.

So to completely fast you need to sit alone in quite a place keeping your eye close without any food, people interaction which is not possible for most people.

The main aim of " fast" is to take control over activities that produce high dopamine and to reconnect with oneself. Remember, dopamine fasting does not going to change the satisfaction level after you go back to your normal day, but this " fast" helps you to reflect on your life- purpose, goals, happiness, relationship, things that are important for you.

The ultimate aim of dopamine fast is to take control over your compulsive behaviour or bad habits.

Reason -:when you stop high dopamine activity then your brain balances brain chemicals, as a result, it tries to find pleasure in small things and try to rewire them. So you will feel good even after doing low or normal dopamine activity like reading books, exercise etc.

2. Taking proper sleep and regular naps -: when you give your brain rest then it tries to balance chemicals in your brain and structure the information. High quality sleep reset and detox our brain from unnecessary data (that we had fed from social media, talks) harmful chemicals which build up during waking hours. Our minds become empty after sleep or nap.

3. Balance your brain chemicals-: Fix the time of your days for social media, YouTube or any other high dopamine activity along with fixed timing for exercise, studying etc. When you schedule everything and repeat it every day then over the period our brain is used to it and can work at peak level with less effort.

Always try to do low dopamine activity before doing high one, you will not lose motivation. In the morning after you wake up with good sleep, your brain already produces dopamine which makes you alert, focused and motivated, so it would be better to do your important task like studying, coding, writing a book etc in the morning time. As time goes on dopamine level goes down which results in less focus, concentration and motivation to do work.

But most of the people around us checks their phone, social media first and spend their morning time on the phone, as a result, their dopamine level suddenly goes high and after spending their morning time when they go to work (studying, coding, writing etc.) their dopamine level goes down, as a result, they are not able to get the same pleasure. But our brain reminds us that previous activity is giving you more pleasure. Due to this they again go back to check their social media to get more pleasure and satisfaction.

Break down your big goal into small pieces(small goals). Allow yourself to celebrate whenever you reach your small goal by giving yourself a healthy snack rather than only celebrating after achieving your big goal. This trick helps your brain to release frequent dopamine and helps you to stick to your path.

Overcome addiction

The whole game of addiction depends upon dopamine. Our brain gets rewired to compulsive indulges in a high dopamine activity without putting any effort. Let's say, someone had an addiction. Addiction is generated when your brain chemicals get misbalanced by performing certain tasks like smoking weeds, porn or any other drugs which suddenly high the level of dopamine.

These addictive substances give very high dopamine suddenly to our brain which normally can't be obtained naturally.

To overcome addiction, you need to decrease the amount of dopamine gradually over the period. Don't try to stop an addiction suddenly because there is the most probable chance that you will fail and feel guilty.

Let's understand with an example -: If you have an addiction to smoking cigarettes and you smoke six cigarettes every day, then over the period reduce its amount. You should move to four then three and after that one and then quit it.

IX

Right approach towards relationship

There are so many books, video on YouTube are present, which teaches you how to get into a relationship with the women/men of your dream.

There are so many relationship coaches who are also doing the same and teaching you a psychological trick and manipulation to get into a relationship.

But, no one teaches you which person is right for you and which person is not suitable for you. Very few people are aware of these fundamentals of relationships.

As a result, there is a large population of people who had stuck into a breakup, toxic relationships and one-sided love. Most teenager nowadays is obsessed over being in a relationship and in the end relationship also end up.

If you are a teenager reading this and in a relationship with someone then, your priority should be your studies and career because at end of the day no one wants to be with someone who is not doing good in his life.

If your partner is not mature enough which would most probably will not support you in your career then getting out of a relationship is the best thing you can do. For teenagers or people in their early twenties, their main should be their career (finances and status), learning new skills, knowledge, right attitude and experiences. If you are doing good in life everyone wants to be with you else no one care about your life.

Let's understand the right approach -: Before getting into a relationship with someone your number one priority should be to know the person very well, checking his/her compatibility with your personality, knowing about his/her beliefs, how they view life, knowing about their past life, their past actions, their past good and bad habits, their habits in current days, how he/she sees you, how he/she behave with the people around you, do he /she congruent, do he/she negotiate, do both of you trust each other or not etc. Even if he/ she had a bad habit in the past does he/she have a genuine willingness to improve in future or not?

How you both are communicating with each other is one of the most important factors to sustain a healthy relationship. Have an open and clear conversation with him/ her about your all wants and desire.

Then you need to make a logical assumption based upon the facts whether this person is right for me or not. You also need to ask yourself how this relationship is going to affect both of you and your upcoming future. Beauty, attractiveness, money, the status of your partner should always be 2nd or 3rd priority when it comes to relationships. The number one reason there have been so many breakups and divorces happen is because most people give a number one priority to physical attractiveness, beauty, money, status etc rather than going through the overall personality of a person.

Also, there is one mistake that is so common is that putting your emotion in a relationship without knowing the person very well, don't put your emotions early. It might give you pain, mental trauma in the future. Don't get into a relationship if you are expecting that another person will give you happiness, love is not about extracting happiness from someone but it's about sharing happiness. For this you need to be already a happy and fulfilled person.

Love is not about suppressing your partner just for your own sake of happiness but it's about growing together in life, both individuals sometimes need to negotiate while making a decision, both individuals should motivate another person to reach their goals of life and act as a support when things are going bad. A relationship should not be your number one priority in life, there is a need to have a life outside of the relationship.

" Her happiness is not my responsibility. She should be happy and I should be happy individually. Then we come together and share our happiness. Giving someone a responsibility to make you happy when you can't do it for yourself is selfish"-: Will Smith

Love is less about romance and more about respect for a person because over a period sometimes you will feel the romance and sometimes not. But respect and compatibility will always be there in a healthy relationship. You need to accept the fact that the attraction, charm in a relationship will fade over time but partnership and compatibility last long.

You should not put your emotion without knowing the person very well, emotion and romance should come later in a relationship.

Signs of secure partner

1. Has respect and admiration -: A secure partner respect and admire their partner without a hero-worship or harsh- criticism. The more secure a partner is with themselves, the more they can witness their partner with kindness, loving intentions and grace.

" Relationships are based on four principles:- respect, understanding, acceptance and admiration"

- Mahatma Gandhi

To have a healthy and great relationship there is a need to have a high level of respect from both partners.

2. Has a clear boundary-: A secure partner has clear and firm boundaries and does not betray themselves or another. Boundaries are our limits. It allows us to have space between the two of you and is the foundation of healthy relationships.

Many of us do not have or understand boundaries because we did not have any modelled clear boundaries from our parent's figures or our boundaries are consistently violated and ignored.

Types of boundaries

• Physical boundaries-: Boundaries around our physical limits and personal space. You and your partner already set boundaries like-:

• Don't kiss me in public places, I feel uncomfortable.

• Even if we had fights, we are not going to get into violence and harm anyone physically.

• You can't force me to have sex with you if I don't feel like doing it.

• Emotional boundaries -: Boundaries around how you feel, who you engage with and what part of yourself you share. Example:

- I am not going to sacrifice my own need to please you.
- Speak up when you feel uncomfortable with how someone is treating you.
- Saying no to your partner when you do not want to do that work or activity.
- I need some quiet time for myself.
- Resource boundaries-: Boundaries around your time and energy. Example: I need some space so that I can spend my time on my hobbies and friends.

While setting boundaries it's normal to feel afraid, guilty and confused. With practice you will be comfortable and does not feel any negativity. How to identify when your boundaries were broken then the answer is to see these signs: discomfort, resentment, stress, anxiety, guilt and fear.

" Emotionally healthy person hold boundaries and respect the boundaries of others. They have the emotional maturity to understand we each have our limits and that those limits are not " mean" or " rude", this feeling comes from co-dependency that is "how you feel about me is how I feel about me." Remember boundary setting is a practice that becomes more comfortable with time".

-: Dr Nicole (psychologist)

Unhealthy boundaries are often characterised by a weak sense of your own identity and your feelings of disempowerment in decision making in your own life.

3. Ability to hear your thoughts and emotions without invalidating them -: A secure partner can hold space for your thought and emotions without denying them or centring their own.

4. Understand their childhood conditioning and how it impacts their patterns of behaviour today -: A secure partner is conscious of their childhood conditioning and actively work to understand their pattern of behaviour.

This allows them to own what is " theirs" rather than projecting and deflecting on their partners. It allows them to openly communicate the reason behind their triggers.

5. Can regulate their own emotions and self soothe healthily – A secure partner can regulate their emotions which allow them to communicate clearly and openly without an unpredictable outburst or shut down(silent treatment). Because they can soothe in healthy ways, they do not use a substance or harmful behaviour to avoid their emotions.

6. Encourage Creativity and self-expression -: A secure partner is not threatened by self-expression and knows that this is an intrinsic human need.

7. Understand their own needs and how to meet them -: A secure partner understands it is not the role of another to meet all of their needs which relieves pressure and resentment between two people.

8. Allow your freedoms and autonomy -: A secure partner honours your autonomy and freedom as well as their own which allows you both room to grow and evolve.

9. Encourages you to spend time alone, with friends, or doing a meaningful activity -: A secure partner values your need for connection, space, self-care and appreciation of your individuality.

Love vs infatuation

The problem in our country is that majority of peoples does not know the true meaning of love and they misunderstood infatuation as love. You might have heard from your friend or people around you – he/she is in love with someone whom they had seen or meet two days ago. The reality is that they aren't in love, they had just developed infatuation.

Even in our cinema industry – you have seen a hero saw the actress and fall in love with her without knowing anything about her just based on her appearance. They had also misrepresented the idea of love and infatuation.

It's a harsh truth that many of us learn about the idea of love and romance from these films. Suppose a person who had grown up watching these films without questioning the reality will going to think that they know what love and romance are because these films had subconsciously rewired our thinking that initial attraction and obsessively thinking about someone is love. I am accepting the fact that initial attraction is necessary but when you enter into a romantic relationship this is not so much important – you will care about the other traits of a person – their personality, behaviour, thinking pattern, priority in life, your compatibility etc.

What causes the development of infatuation?

Let's understand this with an example-: suppose you are a young man (25) and you have seen a girl(22) whom you find attractive- your attraction will be based on her physical attractiveness and also on the way she behaves with you and surrounding. Now when you leave that place and come home or any place you start thinking about her and start feeling butterflies in your stomach. And in the end, you misinterpret this feeling with love. Now, whenever you see this girl again you again feel excited and happy.

Have you ever question why this happen to me? Have you ever question why I found some women attractive and not every woman around? If you have found these answers you will be able to understand what infatuation is?

Now we are going back to the scenario and deconstruct what had happened.

When this man saw this girl he finds her attractive, there are many factors of attraction but we are considering physical attractiveness.

-: from evolutionary psychology, we find someone physically attractive (sexual selection) when a person has these traits

For women-: Glowing and clear skin, high degree of facial symmetry, long lustrous hair, larger eyes, fuller lips, high pitch voice, bright white teeth, narrow waist, long legs, medium-large breasts, wider hips etc. These all traits are attractive because they represent good reproductive health. Men are attracted to these traits because men are designed by nature for evolutionary reasons to look for features that are associated with fertility, youth and good health in women.

For men-: Taller, high degree of facial symmetry, broad shoulders, narrow waist, V-shaped torso, masculine facial dimorphism, a flat abdomen, facial hair- usually stubble beard, thick eyebrows etc. These traits show good reproductive health in men.

Other vital things also include such as whether -:

*he has good social status or not

*he is the resourceful person(money) or not

*he takes responsibility or not

*he has emotional and financial stability or not

* he is well educated and intellectually qualified

* Concept of hypergamy - the action of marrying or forming a sexual relationship with a person of a superior sociological or educational background.

As this woman has qualified with his sexual preference in a partner, this man starts thinking about her. Maybe she had also shown other traits like kindness, independence which make her more attractive in the eye of this man.

When he leaves that place and come back home – he starts thinking about her, this pattern continues for days and week. Let's see what happens in his brain -: whenever this man thinks or see that woman his brain gets flooded by high dopamine, so just thinking about her makes him so much happy as a result he start obsessively start thinking about her and also making stories in his mind. He misinterpreted this happy and excited feeling with love. But in reality, it's known as infatuation.

There might be a chance that this man dates this woman and over the period, he might fall in love but it will take time. Telling this instant feeling of happiness- a love after experiencing butterflies in the stomach will be bullshit. This is very common in our surroundings – people obsessively think and fantasize about the specific the person they like and think that they are in love.

This man does not know anything about women

Now we are going to differentiate love and infatuation so that you can get a clear idea about it-:

• Infatuation is a short-lived attraction for someone and fades over time. It's an intense emotion (mainly based on physical attractiveness) of having them and seeking validation from them.

While in love, you deeply care about someone without feeling the need to own them. You want them to be happy even if they are not with you.

One-sided love

There is another category of a large percentage of people in " one-sided love." It is a feeling of loving someone who does not feel the same for you and keeps living in their fantasy world of imagination. These people develop a crush on someone which is mostly based on physical attractiveness, soft nature towards you etc and they start putting their emotion around the person, without knowing anything (personality, beliefs, behaviour, habits etc) about the person. Many times these people aren't actually in love but they develop infatuation. People who experience one-sided love has hope deep inside them that one day he/she understand his/her love and love him/ her back. It's possible that the person you have fallen for is not exactly your match – he/ she may be too young or too old for you.

This is one of the dumbest things anyone can do because as a result, you are only going to get frustration, depression and pain only, unrequited love will leave you in a loss of hope because you care for someone who doesn't feel the same for you. This unrealistic fantasy is originated in our country from the Bollywood industry, But you need to realize that films and actual real love are so different. In the film, there is only one main character(hero) but in reality, there are so many characters. Romantic rejection will leave a deep emotional scare and research suggest that these people are most vulnerable to the risk of heart attacks.

If you find someone attractive, do not put your emotion first, rather talk to them and try to understand about the personality, beliefs, behaviour etc, and ask them out like would you like to go on date, if he/she accepts then move further, even if you get rejected then accept it because rejection is normal until it is done in an unhealthy way(humiliating fashion)? Accept his/ her decision and have self-respect intact. Do not try to beg anyone and keep in mind that begging someone would not make him/ her love you back. Try to find a new person who is suitable for you.

This will help you to come out of one-sided love-:

- **Make a list of bad things about his/ her**-: When you are in one-sided love, then you are only focusing on the positive quality of his/ her. But we all are human and everyone has something good and bad. Now take a piece of paper and make a list of all negative qualities about his/ her. Never put anyone on a pedestal just because of their beauty/ attractive personality or kind nature towards you, start seeing people as normal humans no one is perfect everyone has some sort of insecurities inside them. Think practically how things are not good.

• **Distance yourself from him/ her**-: As of now you are clear that you can't get into a relationship, but you had already put so much emotion into it. Now it's time to move on and the process will be similar to move on after break up. Disconnect him/ her from your social media, try not to see them, nor ask your friend about his/ her, don't check their profile, delete photo which reminds of him/ her.

• **Focus on your life** -: As you are trying to move on there are the most probable chance is that you are holding a lot of pain and negative emotion inside yourself, now it's time to use that bad emotion to construct your life. Have a clear goal and make a realistic plan, there might be a chance you are preparing for an exam, trying to learn new skills, use that bad emotion as fuel and motivation.

It's time to get busy with your hobbies it could be anything drawing, playing the guitar, cooking, go and join a gym, sports club.

It's time to update yourself, practice meditation, create new healthy habits, eat healthily and cultivate your mind by learning new skills and getting knowledge.

• **Give yourself time to feel grieve** -: Allow yourself to feel the emotion of anger, humiliation, sadness, sorrow. Give yourself few days to be upset. Don't try to suppress bad emotion, let it come out. You can cry, it will make you feel good and help you to free yourself from emotional pain.

- **Open up-:** Share your story with someone whom you trust and get advice from them. This will help you to reduce stress in your mind. Don't suppress your emotion inside you, suppressing emotion may cause you to get into depression, physical pain.
- **It's time for travel and to meet more people** -: Make a plan to go to new places, meet new people, make new friends. This will distract you and by travelling you will realise that there are so many people in this world waiting to meet you and feel proud to be with you and you had just been stuck in your self created bullshit fantasy.
- **Avoid sad songs** -: Avoid all types of songs, films, novels etc which remind you about your crush. Else these songs will remind you about her and also amplify the bad emotions in you which hinder the path of healing.
- **Don't fall for new** -: Learn the lesson from your experiences, do not fall into the one-sided love again.

Understand that relationships are not just built with the effort of one person, there is a need for equal efforts to maintain a healthy relationship.

Even you get so much pain and other bad emotions but the good thing that happens to you is that you get emotionally more strong. You can apply the same steps to move on from break up. Many times especially men puts their " ego" which make things worse.

Think rationally with considering different perspectives without putting your ego, just because he/she had rejected you or don't want to be with you this does not mean that " you have a problem or you're not good enough." Maybe the person who rejected you had a different preference of partner which does not match with you. Accept it and move on.

X
Overcome Shyness

Let me tell you that it's not a problem, every person on this planet has shyness in a different situation. Many people in the world suffer from mild to extreme shyness and are struggling to overcome it. About 20% of shyness is the result of genetic and 80% are due to environmental factors, so the Good thing is that you can change yourself.

Shyness is just a fear of the reaction of getting negative responses (Rejection) from people, so to protect your inner self you become shy over the period. It's an emotion that affects how a person feels and behaves around others. It means feeling uncomfortable, self-conscious, negative self-evaluation and nervous around others.

Why you are shy?

Reacting to new and unfamiliar situations can bring out feelings of shyness, for example – meeting someone new, first day in school or office, talking or speaking in front of the group for the first time. Shyness emerges from self-consciousness, low self-esteem, fear of judgement and rejection.

People are less likely to be shy when they know what to expect from people, have a feeling of security and confidence in what they do or say among familiar people/environment.

Our shyness definition is that " I am not able to talk and express my feeling to certain people so, I am shy." Shyness is stopping you to make new friends, getting into relationships, you will not able to develop leadership skills, social and communication skills which directly means you will suffer if you are too shy.

Apply all these tips to come out of shyness-:

1. Identify your insecurities -: We live in a world where social media plays a huge role in shaping our perspective of perfection and happiness. You will find everyone happy and perfect on social media because nobody posts their failure.

Nowadays, People have become so much obsessed with Instagram models. These models sell body insecurity to most women. Many women are going through plastic surgeries so that they don't lose their beauty. Boys are also obsessed with getting six-pack abs. But the reality is that your beauty will fade over time and you can't maintain six-pack abs for a lifetime, many of them take steroids to maintain them. Don't believe in the bullshit that social media is selling you and stop comparing your life with it. Everyone has some insecurities which can make them uncomfortable. Example- Having small height, bad physique, having darker complex, acne, bad communication skill etc.

If possible work on them such as working on your communication skill, gaining knowledge, taking a proper diet to avoid acne, you will improve if you put in the effort.

Things which you can't change example -:small height, darker complex etc. You need to embrace and accept them and try to be confident in that state. You just need to look presentable.

2. Never say you are shy -: you need to remove the tag of shyness from yourself, never have self-talk that you are shy even if you are. By saying you are shy to people around you, you make them more dominant. As a result, you think you are less confident. There is no need to advertise your shyness.

3. Embrace rejections-: You need to understand that you can't be liked by everyone. You should have a mindset that just getting rejected by 4-5 people does not affect me. There are 7 billion people. You will get rejection so many times, and this is a part of the journey. While getting rejection do not start to think that there is some problem with you and do not take rejection on your ego, just accept it. If you do not accept it then you will again get into negative self-evaluation which will make you shyer.

4. Maintain a confident body language –: Practising confident body language is going to affect your state of mind. Try to use body language, good eye contact etc. Research has found that there is a direct connection between your body language and confidence.

• Take up space -: When you take more space in your environment, this helps you to claim territory and assert your confidence. So instead of crossing your legs or arms try being in normal state.

5. Practice -: You need to push yourself to the situation where you feel shy, if you are shy around girls then try to join a group where you can have a conversation with girls . Don't think too much, just go and start having a conversation, start giving compliments, you need to be more social so, practice public speaking. Try to approach people around you and initiate conversation even the small ones. It will make you more familial in an environment where you feel shy.

"You need to change your experiences, by practising more and more. You will improve."

XI
Power of scheduling

Are you living your life in a boring way going to school, college or office and coming back home and repeating it and not knowing where your life is going and making it more uninteresting without having a purpose and goal in your life?

I agree that you have decided a goal that helps you to move forward in life and grow, even then you can't able to work on them.

To reach your goal, you need to first have clarity about what you want, then you need to break your goals into micro goals on which you work or act every day. When you start scheduling your day according to your priority then you start seeing results and also you get the motivation to work towards your goals. Scheduling is the art of planning your activities so that you can achieve your goals and priorities in the time which is available to you. Scheduling helps you to think about what you want to achieve in a day, a week and month. If you can prepare a clear realistic plan and schedule then your goals will become more tangible. From that, you can see the exact baby steps needed to reach your goal. Scheduling will help you to track your progress, whether you are moving towards your goal or not.

You need to start life with the mindset of an investor. The way you invest your hours of the day whether in positive or negative ways going to affect your upcoming life in a positive/negative way. How to schedule your day? The answer is-

1. Always have a written plan-: When you have written a plan for a day, then your brain gets a clear idea about the task that needs to be done.

So, you need to first make a checklist (even complex task like launching a rocket is done with the help of checklist), according to the priority.

2. Scheduling your day first in the morning or last night -: When you make your checklist before starting your day then you become 25% more effective than the person who does not have a checklist. So, you should have a morning ritual of making a checklist.

3. Have a checklist -: Checklist is a format to verify that all the tasks are done or something got missed and also to verify that all vital tasks are done systematically. Organize your items into categories and the portion of the checklist you are working on should be based on your priorities. Divide your checklist into three parts,

Category 1. -: Vital task. This category should only be dedicated to your goals. The task in this category should be the highest priority.

Example -: Coding for 1 hr, studying for exam etc.

Category 2.-: Necessary task. This task include exercise, meditation etc.

Category 3-: Passive task. This task include watching films, using social media etc. Category one should be done first then second and lastly the third one.

It works because checking items out of a checklist releases a small amount of dopamine that fuels us to take more action, as a result, we end up doing the most task from the checklist. When we feel the effect of dopamine then we become more eager to repeat the same task that gives achievement feeling in the first place.

This is why having a mini goal is an effective way to stay motivated while working for long term goals or big goals. But the items in checklists should be realistic and actual, if you set unrealistic tasks in the checklist then you will feel demotivated to accomplish it. Checklists are required for success, you will avoid serious mistakes, it trains your brain to be more productive and goal-oriented. We need to understand that our brain is designed in a way that it only wants to do the task which is easy and simple and try to avoid complex tasks. Checklist makes our goal simple, easy and clear and avoid our brain from getting into overthinking and give us a command just to execute the next task.

4. Breaks -: You need to have time blocks and breaks because this checklist is done to improve your performance and not to give you stress, also you need breaks for family, relationships and friends. You need to live a balanced life, you just can't focus on one area of your life while ignoring all other areas. Yes, you need to give top priority to your career if you are in your 20s but if you just work and does not give yourself a break then there will be high chances that you hit burnout and feel no motivation to work. Break helps you to de-stress and recharge yourself and make you ready for the next work.

5. Journaling-: At the end of the day you need to evaluate your day, and the best way to do it is by journaling daily. Evaluate how much you accomplish in that particular day and give some reward to yourself if you did all tasks from the checklist. If you miss something, ask yourself why you aren't able to complete tasks, write a genuine reason and also write how you can improve. Journaling helps you to monitor yourself as a mentor and also make you accountable.

XII

Power of emotion

Our emotions have so much power, most people are unaware of this superpower inside them.

Emotion is a strong feeling deriving from one's circumstance, imagination, mood or the people you are with. E- motion also means energy in motion. There are so many emotions we feel like joy, happiness, excitement, fear, anger, sadness, surprise etc.

Life does not go in a smooth flow, we will going to see ups and downs in our life. Sometimes we fail, go through heartbreak, frustration, feeling of love, feeling of achievement and go through so many emotions throughout our life, some good emotions or bad emotions. Humans are emotional creatures and can't work alone for the long term even having a great plan without having emotion.

Most of our behaviour and choices are run by our emotions and feelings.

There have been so many great personalities in history who use their emotions as a weapon in a constructive way to become a much better person and to grow in life.

Let's see examples of them.

1. Dashrath Majhi story:- One day, Falguni (Dashrath Majhi wife) who was heavily pregnant was taking lunch for her husband to the field for which she needed to climb the mountain in the scorching heat. Unfortunately, Falguni's foot got slipped and she fell from the mountain, while hungry Dashrath was waiting for the food. Then someone from the village alerted Dashrath that his wife had fallen from the mountain. Dashrath run into panic and took her blood-splattered wife to the nearest hospital that was 55km away, where she was declared dead.

The heartbroken Majhi who loved his wife more than anything else in the world began cursing the huge mountain and vowed to bring it down to break its ego. In the memory of his beloved wife, determined Majhi took a hammer and a chisel and embarked on a tough and almost impossible mission. He decided to carve out a path so that no other person suffer like her wife. Villagers and even his father reticulated him for challenging a huge mountain. But Majhi was committed to his firm decision.

Dashrath single-handedly carved out 360-feet long, 30-feet high and 30-feet wide passage through the mountain. He made a difference in the lives of villagers by shortening the 55kms distance to 15 km, working day and night for 22 years.

"Sometimes people do great things in love and especially in unrequited love and end up creating history. Taj Mahal is one of the greatest examples of it."

"He has created a powerful source (from love, romance and her memories) that stimulates his creativity, gives access to infinite inspiration and enhances his ambition and being attached to it helps him to be focused.

Her memories were enough to inspire him to greatness."

2. Mahatma Gandhi-: On 7 June 1893, a young barrister, was on his way from Durban to Pretoria. When the train come to a stop in Pietermaritzburg, Gandhi was ordered by the conductor to move from the first-class carriage (reserved for white passengers) where he was sitting to the van compartment for lower class travellers. When Gandhi refused, showing the conductor his first-class ticket, he was forcefully thrown out of the train. "This incident changed the course of his life."

This made him bring a great revolution against racism in South Africa and play a significant role in the independence of India.

" They had removed me from their train. Let them come to my country, I will remove them from my country"

Mahatma Gandhi had mentioned this incident in his autobiography " The story of My Experiments with the truth."

At 26, Rowling moved to Portugal to teach English. There she met and got married to Jorge Arantes. The couple had a child together, but their marriage just did not last long and both got divorced in just one year. Rowling headed back to the UK and write the first Harry Potter book on a typewriter in a cafe. Being a single mother is a struggle in itself, she was also without a job. Her book was rejected by 12 publishers. All of these struggles led her to depression and she wanted to commit suicide but she didn't commited suicide. In 2013, she sold 11 million copies of her new book in 24 hours and becomes the first billionaire author. There are so many great personalities had been in history like Abraham Lincoln, Mother Teresa, Walt Disney etc who were influenced by love, failure, rejection, heartbreak etc and used it to reach greatness.

You might have faced so many emotions of love, heartbreak, rejection, frustration, pain, sadness. Use them as a weapon to level up your life. If you learn the art of transmitting negative emotion(anger, hate, grief and pain) into something constructive or positive then you will become unbeatable "

Remember, Pain is not for suffering. It's for action to level up. Pain gives you two options either you suffer or use it by taking action to level up your life. It's your decision, how you are going to use it.

Many people do not take action when they get bad emotions (pain, rejection etc) and feel frustrated and depressed and to suppress this emotion they end up making bad habits of alcohol, smoking, drugs etc.

"Turn your heart-break into your ambition
Your rejection into your obsession
Your frustration into your drive
Your love into yo.ur inspiration
Your failure into your wisdom"

"When life gives you failure, rejection and pain, first inhale it inside and accept it all. Then try to learn as much as possible from it and again use that emotion as your greatest weapon to level up and grow your life. Turn your wounds into your wisdom. "In the end, let go of all bad emotions else it will affect your physical and mental health badly."

XIII
Multiply your productivity

Being productive in work is one of the most important traits of high achievers. If you see people around you, you will find that they are so much distracted by their phones, social media, notifications etc.

" **Addiction to distraction is the death of creative production**"

:-**Robin Sharma**

If you want to achieve results only 5% of people have achieved then you have to think, produce and behave like only 5%.

We all need to understand that social media like Facebook, Instagram, games like PUBG or any other apps have algorithms & programming designed in a way so that you can spend more and more time in them. Follow all tips to be more productive in your work-:

1. 90-90-1 rule -: It is simple, you are going to spend your first 90minute of your day for 90 days on the single(1) most important game-changing task, in this time you are not going to touch your phone and will be free from technology and distraction. This rule is given by bestselling author Robin Sharma.

Do it until it becomes your habit, you need to do it for a minimum of two months to make it a habit, new research found that it took 66 days to make a behaviour automatic.

As we know, our willpower in the morning is at the maximum, so by using this rule you will be able to do work with the least effort of willpower. When you do it first in the morning, you will become so much motivated to accomplish more work and you will gain momentum. For most of us, it's a marvellous period as we are most energetic and focused.

Example- If you are a student, then you will be studying any topic of your book or if you are an entrepreneur then it can be working on an idea, for a musician it will be practising playing an instrument. If you introduce this rule and become consistent with it then you will notice that your productivity, efficiency, creativity have increased exponentially.

The problem with most people is that they are not aware of their most productive times. As a result they waste their effective time doing less valuable things or even waste it with people, entertainment just for the sake of instant gratification. But those who understand it and use their productive period effectively are able to do the difficult task in less time.

2. Environment of total focus-: If you look at the average performer then you will find that they rarely have cared for the environment.

They get distracted by their phone, social media, noise, toxic people etc.

We live in a world where the focus is more important than your intelligence

To achieve any significant result, you need to be a focused person. Research has found that our environment plays a significant role in influencing your behaviour, motivation to act and mood.

Work in place of no distraction / least distraction or work in solitude, organise your working environment with important things only.

· Lightning: Use room with bright light (natural or artificial) as it improves mental health and helps us to stay away from depression, sleep and anxiety.

· Temperature- Increase in temperature leads to aggression while a decrease in temperature leads to depression so, have a suitable room temperature according to your need. Not too cold nor too warm.

· Colors: The Colors of your working space (room, office etc) will going to affect your mood and emotions. You might not even notice it but your mind and body have a response to seeing Colors. Bright Colors make you feel energized. We all usually want relaxation, so for this choose Colors like sky blue, violet, light pink, light green, white, light yellow.

When we feel stressed out we subconsciously look for the blue colour, we might look up to the sky or we might see seawater and we do a bit of daydreaming to calm down. Looking to blue colour releases chemicals in the body that promote calmness.

3. Choose your friends / social group really-really well
-: Science and research found that the number one way to improve your performance is to surround with the same mindset people who are also high achievers. We usually hear we are an average of 5 people around us that is a fact because people around us indirectly influence our attitude,

perception to view the world, consciousness and behaviour and these are the things that directly influence our quality of life.

You might be a very productive person in your group of friends, but if you are constantly surrounded by pessimistic friends, have low consciousness, always talks negatively and have no vision for life then it will impact who you eventually become, your productivity will go down, your achievements in life will get affected directly.

Example-:

· If you are in a group of 5 people and all your four friends like to smoke, then there is a most probable chance that you will also start smoking in the future if you continue to hang out with them.

· If you want to lose 15 kg weight to get into shape and you constantly hang out with fat person having bad fitness and does not care about what they eat then it will be very hard for you to lose 15 kg. But if you constantly hang out with health-conscious people then it will be easy for you to lose 15 kg because everyone in the group was motivated and committed to being healthy. If you hang out with a successful, optimistic person then, you are unconsciously without being aware of, creating a path for success and happiness in life. Many people do not believe it, but it's a real truth, if you do not believe it then take a piece of paper and write down the name and salary of four people with whom you hang out the most and then find the average of the salary of this four individual, you will see that the average of salaries is similar to your salary. This applies to almost all parts of our life from achievement, income, happiness, health etc.

The important question is how to find the right group of people?

First, take a piece of paper and write down about your future life, what you want to achieve, how much your income should be, how your health will look like, what type of relationship you want etc. Then look at your current friends group and analyse where they are serving your future life or not. If they do then its good, continue to hang out but if it doesn't then cut them out from your life, go and find new people with the same mindset as you, find those who are hungry to achieve high and willing to work for achieving greatness.

If you have not found people with a successful mindset then it's better to be alone rather than hanging out with people with no vision for life, no goals, no ambition and also having bad habits. All clever and high performer people are aware of it, so they do not hang out with low performers just to protect their mindset and consciousness. Do not hang out with people who do not force you to grow in life and are comfortable in being mediocre.

Choose your friends wisely they are going to impact your future so much.

4. Learn simplicity -: Successful businessman, sports player, musician, high achiever believe in "simplicity." They do few task daily which is most important and does not fill their day with so many tasks. Complexity leads to confusion, the problem with most people is that they are able to create a plan but when the time for execution comes they get confused with so many tasks, which results in a lack of clarity and affects performance and productivity.

" Stop fooling yourself being busy with being productive"

Co-founder of Google said, "Success will come from simplicity". Most people fill their life with so many goals at a time due to this focus get diversified and as a result, they were not able to achieve whatever they want. Study world-class experts in any field – athlete, artist, scientists, CEOs and you will discover one characteristic that runs through all of them- focus. The reason is simple, you can't be great at one task if you are constantly dividing your time into ten different works.

Try to live your life in simplicity, try to fill your daily routine with the most important tasks and eliminate the passive tasks for later.

5. Take care of your health -: Productive people are mostly aware of their health because a sick mind & body can't work effectively. So they usually take care of what they do, their sleep and exercise. Never take your health for granted because it's the most valuable asset you have ever got. Most people in our country ignore it and understand it's important when it's too late. The food that you eat and the quality of your sleep directly impact your performance. You can't be a high performer with a sick mind and body.

6. Having a checklist-: Complex task like putting a man on the moon, launching a rocket, doing open-heart surgery become simple just using a checklist, then why not use in our daily life to accomplish our task.

At the beginning of the day make a priority checklist for the day.

If you don't make a checklist then there will be most probable chance that you will waste your time doing a task that is not valuable.

There is another major reason so many people procrastinate is that they are waiting for the time when there will be no problems in their life. But the actual reality is that this will not going to happen there will always be some big and small problems in our life. Example – having some form of family issue, relationship issue such as break up, maybe you are working in a toxic office environment where you feel that your energy is drained, maybe you are fighting with a friend, maybe some people don't like you, some people are spreading bad rumours about you etc.

You will always be going to have ups and downs in your life, no one can escape from it.

But the actual problem starts when you start to think that until this problem is solved, I will not going to prepare for my competitive exam or work on goals and my dreams.

For example- you might have seen your friend to stop preparing for the exam due to a breakup. These things are very common if you observe your environment. But you need to have a mindset that no matter what the problems I am going through, I will always put my goals and dream as a priority especially when you are from (16-32 years of age) else you will get into the state of low self-esteem and frustration. Don't waste your energy, time and focus on things that will not going to serve you and in addition going to give you stress, take ownership of your life.

I am not telling you to ignore the problem or not to fix them, but I am telling you not to make that problem/ issue your top priority.

Always ask yourself that – is this problem (breakup, fight with friends etc) going to matter in next five years, if not then why to stress over it. The majority of people concentrate and focus on bullshit issues that they were going through and make the core of their life and stop and forget about their long term goals and dreams of their life. Don't be in that category.

" If it's not gonna matter in next 5 years – don't spend more than 5 minutes being upset about it."

XIV

Gratitude

The best way anyone can live his life is by being happy, satisfied and grateful. No matter how much money and resources you have, in the end nothing is going to matter if you are not happy within yourself. The reality is that we all are focusing on the things that we don't have in our life (more money, career etc), don't take me wrong it's important to progress in life and strives for a better quality of life. But the problem is that we do not appreciate the thing that we already have in our life (Health, relationships etc).

There are so many examples out there in the world where people first sacrifice their health to earn more money and when they have accumulated a good amount of money, that same money is spent on their health later in life. The problem with most of us is that we take things for granted and when we lose them then we understand their value in our life.

The best way to appreciate the things that you already have had is by being grateful. Gratitude is a feeling of thankful appreciation of all that's good in your life. We feel happy because when we are focusing on the things that we already have in our life rather than thinking and focusing on things that we don't have. Whether we say " thank you" to someone or receive the same from others, the feeling it brings is pure satisfaction, encouragement and happiness. Expression of gratitude helps in building and sustaining long term relationships. When we express gratitude and receive the same our brain release neurotransmitter dopamine and serotonin which make us feel good and enhance our mood immediately.

Benefits of gratitude -:

1) **Happiness** -: Those who practice gratitude consistently feels better about themselves and the people around them. They positively impact their own life and the life of people around them compared to the person who does not practice gratitude.

2) **Positivity** -: Practising gratitude helps in decision-making skills, self-care and helps the person evolved as a new attractive person. People who practice gratitude are less likely to compare themselves with others as they appreciate their quality and also have an optimistic view towards life. These people know that everyone is unique and special in themselves.

3) **Health** -: Gratitude has so many physical and mental health benefits such as less body pain, improve sleep quality, enhance the CELL-MEDIATED immune system – the way our body fight bacteria and viruses, reduce stress hormone like cortisol by 23%, protect the heart by decreasing the blood pressure. In addition to that, grateful people are found to avoid smoking and tobacco thus, they are away from addictive bad habits. Research has found that grateful peoples are more likely to exercise and spend an average of 36% more exercising per week and thus have overall better health. Also, have psychological benefits like-:

- Improve self-esteem and overall mood.
- More emphatic and less aggressive even after facing negative experience.
- Reduce toxic and traumatic emotions like envy, resentment, regret etc.

4) Relationship-: Gratitude has immense positive benefits in relationships. Those who practice gratitude have more satisfaction in relationships, more love and respect for people around them. They don't have negative feelings of jealousy.

" Gratitude creates the most wonderful feeling. It can resolve disputes, strengthen friendships and makes us better man or women"-: Gordon Hinkley

Gratitude in work – Grateful worker is more efficient, more productive and more responsible. Expressing gratitude will help you to build interpersonal bonds and triggers a feeling of closeness and bonding. 5) Depression -: Those individuals who consistently practice gratitude are at low risks of depression and even if they are already in the depression then they recover much more faster compared to ungrateful individuals.

Individuals who practice this ritual are reported to be less angry and aggressive and have much more patience.

" It is impossible to feel grateful and depressed in the same moment"-: Naomi Williams

Ways to be grateful in life-:

1) Maintain a gratitude journal -: Maintain a small journal, every day before going to sleep write 3 things you are grateful/thankful for that day. In this way, you are programming your brain to focus more on positivity and even if you are facing a tough time this will help you to be optimistic and also protect you from getting into depression.

2) Surround yourself with visual reminders -: place a photo of your loved ones or any beautiful memory in the places where you spend your most time, it could be your room, office etc. Our brain wants proof to make solid beliefs. So when you place photographs you are telling your brain, yes I have this people/ memory for which I can feel grateful. By doing this you are sending conscious and regular signals to your brain to attract happiness and abundance.

3) Appreciate yourself -: Appreciate positive quality of yourself like being honest, showing kindness, your curiosity to learn, ambition, believe in yourself etc. This will boost your self-esteem and feel your motivation to take more positive actions.

4) Appreciate 3 people in your life -: When you are grateful for someone , then you create a positive vibe in a relationship. Choose three people, it could be your mother, father, sister, your partner, friend etc. Appreciate their support and positive impact on your life.

5) Carry a physical token of gratitude -: whenever you encounter a physical token of gratitude like stone, locket, ring etc then whenever you touch or see them it will remind you to practice gratitude.

6) Appreciate the smallest of the blessings -: If you have a house to live, clothes to wear and always have food on plates then you should be thankful for it because you are better off than 75% of the world population. There are so many people on this planet who are not able to get even three times of food every day, but most of the time we all take these blessings for granted but don't be that person.

There is no fixed rule to practice gratitude, some people do not want to practice in a fixed routine as they get bored(like daily gratitude journaling). That's okay, there is no meaning of practising gratitude if it does not come from within your heart, but you will see the magnificent results of the practice of gratitude in a very short time.

" Remember gratitude is one of the shortest paths to happiness"

XV
Art of fortune creation

Everyone wants money in his life to survive in this world. We are living in a materialistic world, where most of our resources and comfort depend on money. There are some fundamental rules of money and most people are not aware of it, thus there is the problem of lack of money and poverty. Some people are aware of it as a result they hold a huge amount of wealth.

Rule no. one(Mind-set) -:The way you think about money can have a huge influence on your ability to create wealth. A poverty mindset is a mindset that people develop over time based on their belief that they will never have enough money or there is no money in a market that they can have. Most people have wrong associations with money, they think that money is the root cause of all evil but in reality that is wrong. The truth is lack of money and attachment with money is the root cause of all evils. But we need money to manage our life properly. You need to have your own strong positive belief about money, this is the first step in the path of wealth creation. How can you have fortune if you have so much negativity associated with it, our society (friends and family) had shaped a wrong mindset that you need to change. Usually, there is a major difference in the mindset of rich people and poor people in addition to that they have a different perspective to see the world.

Some of these mindset differences are -:

• Rich mindset seeks to spend their time, energy and resources on work that continues to pay off long after the effort has been invested. They try to create a system that automatically generates value.

While a poor mindset seeks short- term return like hours for money as they think that resources invested without instant return are wasted. Mostly they seek instant gratification.

• Rich mindset understands that he can never know everything, so he consistently tries to learn from others, from other people success and failure. He knows that the more he learns, the more he earns.

While, poor mindset believe that he knows everything, as a result, he shut down doors for gaining new knowledge, skill from the world.

• Rich mindset understands that the first goal is to gain a surplus of resources, then to use that resource to accelerate things like education, business etc.

While a poor mindset sees resources instantly as an opportunity for consumption and exaggerates lifestyle.

• Rich mindset always looks for opportunities to grow their wealth, learn something new (skill, knowledge and attitude)

While a poor mindset does not.

• Rich mindset does not afraid of failure and taking risks, they are aware that failure is part of a journey, which comes to teach something. They know that risk is important in life to reach higher altitude. There are no successful people who had accumulated wealth without taking a risk in their life. They know that growth does not happen in their comfort zone.

While poor mindset has a fear of being judged after a failure, so most of them never try something new and do not take any risk in life.

• Rich mindset build multiple sources of income while a poor mindset just focuses on only one source of income.

• Rich mindset believes in saving, investing and multiplying their money while poor mindset splurge on materialistic things.

• Rich mindset believes that "I create my life" while poor mindset believes "life happens to me".

• Rich thinks big while poor thinks small.

• Rich says that "expand your means" while poor says "live below your means".

Rule number two (financial education) –: Rich people know the importance of financial education to create wealth. Financial education is the ability to understand how money works. It the art of investing, saving and multiplying money. According to the survey, more than 75% of adult in our country does not have the basics of financial education. Most people do not know how to manage their money, the difference between assets and liabilities, how to spend money, how to invest etc.

Let's understand some basics -:

1) Difference between asset and liability -: Asset is a resource that you or your company hold which can provide you with future economic benefits and liability is a resource that you hold which provides you with future economic losses. In short, asset puts money in your pocket and liability takes money out. Rich people spend their money on assets and focus on creating passive income (money earned on an investment or work completed in the past that requires little or no active involvement to generate ongoing revenue) from it. Examples-: running a blog, YouTube channel, renting out the property while when poor mindset get money they spend their money every time on buying liabilities example buying new phone, TV and spend in luxuries. Rich people spend on luxuries by developing more sources of income to compensate for it.

One reason many people are in financial trouble is that they get confused over liabilities with assets. For example: many people think that their house is an asset when it's a liability. A simple definition of an asset is to put money in your pocket while liability takes it out.

2) Types of incomes -: There are three types of the way people earn money.

• If you have a job and receives a paycheck then you make money from earned income. When you are earning from a paycheck, you are exchanging time for money. Example-: a web designer, police officer, a grocery store cashier.

Benefit-: you can earn as much faster compared to the next two incomes.

Drawback -: you have to sacrifice your time to receive it and the earned income has a high rate of taxes compared to the other two incomes.

• If you make money through sales of capital gains, you make money from capital gain income. For Example -: when someone buys stock in a corporation at a given price, they plan to sell the same stock at a higher price in the future. So if they buy stock of $20 today, and the price goes up to $70 when they sell that stock, they make $50 in capital gain.

Captain gain= selling price- purchase price

Benefit-: It's mostly passive, you don't require to do active work to obtain capital gain income and this type of income taxed more favourably than earned income

Drawback-: It requires you to have existing money to invest in assets like bonds, stocks etc.

• Passive income -: This is income that you earn from owning assets that require no work on your part. Example -: Rental property, owning website etc

Benefit -: You do not have to sacrifice your time to own it, instead, the assets that you own can produce income for you while you are sleeping.

Drawback-: same as capital gains, requires money to generate it.

3. Savers are losers -: The reason savers are losers because the value of the rupee continues to lose its value because of inflation. Basically what's your money can buy in the future is less than it can purchase now. You need to make money at a much fast rate than inflation to be rich and retire comfortably.

The best way to protect your money is to buy assets from that money.

4. Budgeting-: Building and maintaining a budget is an essential factor of personal financial success. It is the roadmap for your finances. Budgeting is the process of creating a plan to spend your money, it is important because it ensures that you always have enough money for the things you need and things that are significant to you. It is simply balancing your expenses with your income, if you do not balance and spend more than you earn then you will have problems. Rich people use budgeting as a way to generate more income and expending their standards so that they can expand their expenses to afford whatever they desire. Everyone spends but building wealth depends upon spending less than you earn. That's where the budget can help you to sort out your needs from your wants which helps you to make a better decision, budget track your all spending pattern. Many people buy a new phone, electronic gadgets whenever something new comes in the market, they end up buying something that is not crucial as a result they lose their money.

Pay yourself first mean that enough income is saved or invested before monthly expense made. You should pay your savings and investment accounts first. Example-: paying into a health saving account, paying off debts, creating an emergency fund, saving to invest in your personal growth by learning a skill, buying books, buying a course etc. When you pay yourself first, you are prioritising your financial well being. Your expenses can be broken down into two parts-:

• Mandatory expenses -: Bills that must be paid like rent, electric bills, things that you need to live, healthy good foods and medicines etc.

• Optional expenses-: It includes expenses for entertainment, travel, new phone, TV etc.

When you only save what is left at the end of the month, you are putting saving to the second category:- optional expenses which vary every month. If you think about your saving after everything else is paid, then most probably you will end up having no money to save.

There is one famous rule for budgeting – the 50/30/20 rule

According to this rule Divide your income into three categories and allocate 50% of income to your needs, 30%

on wants and 20% to saving and investments.

Let's understand why budgeting is important -:

1) Budget helps you to make investment and track them.

2) Budget expose you to your excessive spending behaviour.

3) Budget helps you to set financial goals and achieve them.

4) Budget helps you to become aware of your income deficiencies which helps you to recharge them.

Concept of cash flow

Why only certain groups of people only able to get rich?

Why 10% of people in the world hold 90% of wealth and why 90% of people hold only 10% of the wealth? Why a certain group of people can get financial freedom in their 30s and why the majority of people does not have enough money to live their desired life. The answer to all this question is hidden in the "concept of cash flow"

The concept of cash flow is explained by Robert Kiyosaki in his famous book " cash flow quadrant".

The cash flow quadrant represents the different methods by which income is generated. Different methods of income require different technical skills, educational paths and different types of people.

Our society is divided into four categories of people's depending upon the work they do.

1. Employees -: They have a job
2. Self employees -: They own the job
3. Business owners-: They own a system
4. Investors-: They make their money work for them.

1) Employees -:Majority of people in our society comes under this quadrant. For this group job, security is more important than financial freedom.

The reason why most people's works employees quadrant because most of us are programmed to do this from childhood. We get a suggestion from society(parents, friends, family, schools) that " study hard, get a high paying job and have a secure future". Very few parents advise their children about starting a business and investing.

There is nothing wrong with having job security it's all your choice. But it's your choice, do you want job security or financial freedom. Although you can become rich working in this quadrant, it's quite tough compare to other quadrants. Example-: Google employees.

2) Self employees-: These types of people own a job and usually like to work on their own. The mindset of people in this quadrant is that "if you want to do it right, you have to do it by yourself."

They trade their time for money. They have to devote more time to earn more. They think that their freedom is more important than financial freedom.

Examples -: doctors, lawyers, shop owner etc.

3) Business owners -: This type of people create a system for consistent income with the help of people. They make people work for them. One of the best for accumulating wealth.

They do not trade their time exchange for money. Even in his absence, their employees will work for them.

4) Investors-: They are the most financially free groups and they make their money work for them.

They invest in businesses, real estate, stocks etc.

These types of people has usually free time and freedom as compared to any other quadrant as they do not need to actively participate in creating income.

There is a difference in the core values of people's

- People on the left side of the quadrant choose security, while people on the right side of the quadrant choose financial freedom.
- Left side is owned by employees and self employees, while the right side of the quadrant is owned by business owners and investors.
- On the Left side of the quadrant it's difficult to get rich, while on the right side of the quadrant it's easy to become rich.
- Left side of the quadrant consists of 90% of people's with less than 10% of the wealth while the right side of the quadrant consists of 10% of people's with more than 90% of the wealth.
- People on the left side of the quadrant trade time for money while on the right side of the quadrant people's money does not depend on time.

"It's possible to become rich in all four quadrants or remain poor in any."

You do not need to entirely shift to another quadrant at once, you can keep your feet in two or more quadrants.

Example-: If you are an employee then you can jump on the right side and start making investments.

Employee+ investor

Business owner+ investor

Self employee+ investor

But the best way to get rich is when you are on the right side of the quadrant. i.e. business owner+ investor. To make a change in the quadrant, you need to learn skills, knowledge, having an attitude that is required in that particular quadrant else you will fail.

Investment -: To become prosperous financially it's important to do investments. Most people are afraid of investing because most of us does not have proper knowledge about investing. Before starting an investment you need to have proper knowledge, about what you are doing.

" *The most important investment you can make is in yourself*"- *Warren buffet*

Find out which assets group excite the most and first learn how to make an investment in that group, study successful people of that group to find out how some people able to make a profit and what cause losses, then only put your time, money and energy into that group. This group can be stocks, real estate, Bitcoin etc.

There are simple step to create a winning investment plan

• First determine how much you can invest-: Most people make excuses that they do not have money to start investing which is not simply true. Instead, they spend their money on buying numerous unnecessary things, the problem is not that they do not have enough money but the problem is how they budget.

You need to invest a priority, find out how much money do you want to invest each month.

• Find out what you want to invest in -: In what assets you want to make investments.

1. It could be paper assets like stocks, bonds, mutual funds etc.

2. It could be real estate where you get income from rental property or by gaining capital from selling and buying property.

3. It could be commodities like metals(gold, silver, copper), food(grains, coffee, sugar). Commodities are future gain (or loss) investment, where you buy the commodity in the hope to gain future profit.

- Once you know how much to invest and where to invest, establish a long term investment goal.

XVI
Rituals that will change your life

Most of your life problems will fade away if you will have a fixed time to wake up in the morning and also have a fixed time to go to sleep at night.

First, understand why I am telling you to wake up early?

Do waking up early has something to do with success. The answer is NO. There are the majority of successful people and rich people who love to wake up early and also there are many successful people who work till late at night (3-4 AM).

Success has nothing to do with timing but everything to do with your focus, habits and choices.

But waking up early in the morning have some advantage over those who work till late night as rising early gives better result for your health(including mental & physical), your emotional state and your spiritual state(happiness & calmness).

But the question is how to wake up early?

To wake up early, first, you need to sleep on time.

Fix the amount of time you want to sleep and does not change the pattern (timing) then only you will feel fresh and more energetic every day.

Decide how much sleep do your body needs according to the work you do, it may be 6hrs, 7hrs or more, you can't neglect the importance of sleep. Develop a small night ritual that helps you to prepare for sleep, having a nightly ritual is as important as a morning ritual. Ritual is a pattern of behaviour regularly performed in a set manner.

Night ritual -:

1. Put off all the screens (phone, TV, laptop etc) just 60 min before sleep. The blue light emitted by phone/ laptop screens restrains the production of melatonin a hormone that controls the internal clock/sleep-wake cycle (circadian rhythm), blue lights suppress melatonin, as a result, you experience insomnia and tiredness the next day. Blue lights from our screens are artificial colours that mimic daylight and our body is not able to differentiate between natural light and artificial light.

We are living in a world full of distractions from social media and its notification, phone Apps are designed in such a way so that the user spends more and more time in it. Checking our phone psychologically engage us, make us more active and alert by stimulating the brain.

Do not watch TV before sleep, most people watch the news before they sleep which is the worst thing you can do before sleep because our subconscious mind is active before sleep and you put negative news (thought), as a result, you become a pessimistic person day by day.

2. Read a book of affirmation or any good book, you can do journaling in which you can analyse your whole day or you can make plans for the next day. Choose physical books and avoid reading on your screen. Many people's find

that reading before their bedtime is one of the best ways to wind down and also allows you to gain new knowledge and information. There are some benefits of reading before bedtime -:

- It reduces stress-: Throughout the day we go through a series of works which also builds stress, and if we try to sleep in that state then most probably we will not able to get high-quality sleep, so by immersing yourself with a good book you will able distract your brain from stress, worries and tension, research had found that reading for just six minutes reduces stress up to 68%. Reading also allows your muscle to relax and slow down your breathing, leaving you in a calm state.

- It boosts brainpower-: Our brain is a muscle too, and just like any other muscle in our body it needs to work out to keep it healthy and strong. Reading is a neurologically challenging task because while reading our brain is simultaneously engaged in visualisation, analysing data, processing information etc.

This means that reading is a great way to work out the brain in a fun way. People who engage their brain in activities like reading, solving puzzles or playing chess are 2.5 times less likely to get into mental illness like Alzheimer's.

- It improves your emphatic skill-: Reading makes you a more emphatic person. Empathy is the ability to understand other people's emotions and feelings. While reading fiction books(novels), we see the world with someone else's eyes or with someone else point of view which train our minds to apply this skill in real life.

- It boosts creativity-: Reading broadens our imagination by stimulating the right side of our brain. It literary open our mind to new possibilities and ideas. Without imagination people aren't able to come with new inventions and ideas, imagination encourages innovative and creative thinking. Reading affirmation before sleep helps you to reprogram your subconscious mind, as we know the subconscious mind govern 90% of behaviour and attitude. So programming your mind helps you to achieve your goals, become much happier and fulfilled. Create your affirmation and write them down, it helps you to reprogram your limiting or destructive believes into constructive ones, the affirmation will help to change desire into a burning desire.

Just repeat your desire 20-30 times with emotion and vision, you will get a great desire to accomplish your goal or dream. Very few people are aware of this " power of repetitive sentences". It has the power to heal you from past mental traumas, cure anxiety and depression, improve self-esteem etc.

Example -: I believe I can do anything.

I can accomplish anything I focus on.

I will be fearless today.

I am worthy.

I see challenges in my life as an opportunity to grow.

I am proud of who I am becoming.

3. Have a clean environment in your bedroom and put lights off as light affects the melatonin and affects the quality of sleep. Artificial light mimics natural light which keeps you away from sleep. One of the best things is to eliminate all the lights and get heavy curtains to eliminate outside light. Use light colour bed sheets like sky blue, baby pink, white etc which help you to sleep in a calm environment. Take care of the temperature of your bedroom, general suggested temperature of the bedroom should be between 60-67 degrees Fahrenheit. The bedroom

should be cool (moderate or refreshing state) but not cold. Heat exposure increases alertness and decreases slow-wave sleep, rapid eye movements which results in bad sleep quality.

Our brain associates places and things with our behaviour, example -: you might be wondering why you feel the urge to study when you sit near your study desk, the reason behind it is your brain associated study desk with studies, so when you see desk it acts as a trigger to your brain for study. In the same way, if you repeatedly go to your bed only for sleep, then it becomes easy to sleep. But most of the time we do random things like watching movies while sitting in bed, playing video games in our bed, as a result, our brain develops triggers for playing video games or watching films whenever we sit on the bed which results in the delay of sleep.

Morning ritual:-

1. Reading -: Fill your brain with positive thoughts. Read and gather new knowledge. Read a good book on different subjects such as business, spirituality, health etc. It's a perfect time to cultivate your mind. Focus and concentration- as we are living in a digital world of screens, the attention span of normal people have reduced so much. Apps in our phones rewire our brains for instant gratification. But we all know the importance of delayed gratification, focus and concentration for success. When you read a book in the morning for 30-60 minutes, then you are training your brain to increase its focus and concentration muscle. This ritual helps you to become a focused person for the whole day.

2. Listening to uplifting music -: Music directly impact our psychology and perception to view the world. If you install a habit of daily listening to uplifting music which

stimulates positive emotions, calming music that touches your soul and encourages you to grow, appreciate and be grateful then you will feel motivated, energized and happy for the rest of the day.

3. Exercise -: When you do exercise in the morning, you will become more active and feel energetic the whole day. Just for 20min form a ritual of running or any exercise. Exercising in the morning will increase blood flow and release a hormone endorphin which triggers positive feeling and reduce the perception of pain. It will maintain a high energy level for the whole day and help you to cope with stress, anxiety and depression. It builds your mental strength to face obstacles in life, while doing exercise you push your limits which rewire your brain to push yourself out of your comfort zone and persist when things get hard in life, which indirectly helps you to become successful.

4. Scribing -: It means journaling. It is a great way to process your thought and help you to be more self-aware and clear about your goals, you will also able to plan your day. Writing down your most important task in the morning helps you to be more focused on the essential task. It helps you to provide and manage your time in a better and effective way. As a result, you simplify your life by giving focus and energy to what counts for your overall life progress.

5. Meditation-: This is one of the best mindfulness techniques you can have, it will make you happier, will give inner peace and satisfaction. It will help you to make good decisions in life and will make you emotionally stable.

Choose any few things mentioned above, you will feel blissful.

Health and healthy circadian rhythm

A very vast majority of people on this planet spend their half of their life fighting with chronic diseases like cancer, diabetes, Alzheimer, cardiovascular disease etc. But if you can understand the concept of circadian rhythm many of us can prevent, manage and can cure many chronic diseases. So let's understand what is circadian rhythm?

It is a 24-hour cycle through which our body goes through which tell our body when to wake up, when to sleep ,when to eat and when to secrete hormones in our body. Almost every plant and animal do have a circadian rhythm which is controlled by what we call the circadian clock. This clock is encoded in our DNA.

How do we know that circadian clocks are inbuilt? Example- If we lock someone in a house with no clue about the outside time then his/her circadian clock will make him sleep somewhere around 10 O'clock and will have a deep sleep around 2 O'clock and wake up at 5-6 AM. As soon as he wakes up in the morning his body starts decreasing melatonin hormone and cortisol level start rising which make him alert. His peak performance time will be in the noon and the evening melatonin levels start rising more and more. Again somewhere around 10 PM, he sleeps and this cycle continues. Almost every single gene is on and off at different times of the day-night cycle. Every single brain chemicals and hormones also rise and fall at a different time of the day-night cycle.

So to have a healthy circadian rhythm is to have good health.

If we move any human or animal to another planet that has identical conditions similar to earth but have a different day-night cycle other than 24 hours cycle then we cannot easily survive on that planet. So from this, we can understand the importance of having a healthy circadian rhythm.

But many of us disrupt this rhythm and stay late up at night doing late-night assignments or work and the next day feels horrible. When we continue abusing our circadian rhythm for a long time likes weeks and month then the chance of having chronic diseases will be very high.

Almost every single organ and even cell do have their clocks. What does it mean that our brain is most effective in solving a complex problem in the middle of the day and also need rest at night. Similarly, every organ has its own peak performance time at a certain time of the 24-hour cycle and every organ need sleep so that it can refresh. All the clocks in our body for different organs work together to give us circadian rhythm(which regulates sleep, metabolism and our mood).

Circadian rhythm is connected to the outside world by two mediums- **sunlight and timing of food.** Just getting day sunlight and taking food at proper timing will help us to get back to a natural rhythm. Food at the wrong timing will affect your sleep quality in a bad way.

One interesting question arises how does sunlight influence our circadian rhythm? our eyes have a blue light sensory protein known as Melanopsin and when sunlight is rich in blue light when falls into our eyes then it sends signals to our brain that it's day outside, as a result, our body release cortisol which makes us feel alert.

But these protein is less sensitive to orange lights, so in the evening blue lights are low, it sends our brain that it's dark outside as a result melatonin levels start rising which make us feel sleepy.

When we use our phones and devices (which have blue lights) in the evening or night it confuses our brain that it's still day outside due to this our body produces less melatonin causing difficulty in sleeping, poor sleep quality and insomnia. So it is advised not to use the screen before bedtime and to use orange light mode on your screens while using in the evening/ night.

XVII
Mentor

Everyone wants to become successful in whatever career they have chosen, some want to build a multimillion-dollar company, some want to be a doctor, singer, athlete etc. But most of the time people are not able to achieve their desired goals and even though if they have achieved the goals they took too much time just because of a lack of knowledge and guidance in that particular field. But if a person takes guidance, advice and knowledge from a person who is good in that particular field then there is a more probable chance that he/ she will be able to achieve his/ her goal in a decided time frame. A mentor should be someone who had already achieved greatness and have deep knowledge and experience in a particular field. Also, he/she should have the willingness to share his wisdom with another person. The problem with most people is that they usually take advice from wrong people(not having experience and knowledge in a particular field), it could be your family and friends etc.

  How can you take advice on starting a business from your father who never started any business, how can you take financial advice from your friend who is in poverty.

Here I am not telling you that your family and friends are wrong (have love and respect for them). They are giving the knowledge that they have. You are wrong here because you are not taking advice from the right person. You should take advice from someone who has already achieved the things that you want to achieve. For example – suppose you want to earn 30 crores in 1 year then you should take advice and mentorship from someone who had already achieved it, they can give you the actual path needed to achieve the goal.

Most of us ignore the importance of mentors as a result they end up wasting a lot of time. Athletes and sports players know the importance of having a mentor to achieve a result, but it should not be limited to just one field. Whatever goals you have, try to find experts in that field and take advice and learn from them. Find a mentor for career goals, health goals, spiritual goals etc. If you want to crack any exam find the right person to guide you. 80% of CEOs say that they received some form of mentorship. Business is twice as to survive if the owner has a mentor. The mentor should be someone who must respect his mentee, appreciate uniqueness of the mentee, always be honest and should also listen to the opinion of the mentee without judging him or destructive criticising. Every successful person in the world whether they are an entrepreneur, musician, athletes

All had a great mentor who helped them to unlock their potential.

The reason why you should have a mentor -:

• **Right knowledge** -: we all know that to become better at something, we need to have the right knowledge in that particular field. When you are with a mentor you will learn and gain new knowledge which ultimately helps you to grow. Many times we get confused because of wrong knowledge especially when you are preparing for the exam, there is so much confusion such as what to study and what not to, how to practice problem effectively, how to study a certain topic etc. All these problems can be easily solved if you are in touch with a mentor(a person who already cracked the exam).

This same rule applies to all other fields such as starting a business, practising for football matches etc.

• **Unbiased feedback** -: An ideal mentor will think critically and give advice without falling into bias and manipulation. Without a mentor, you will end up making the wrong choice because of a lack of experience. Also, there is a probable chance if you don't have a mentor you will take advice from a random person and chances are that your thoughts get biased and manipulated.

• **Constructive criticism** -: A right mentor will criticise you constructively and tell you openly about your mistakes and how to fix them without judging you. He will tell you about your weak points without any hesitation because most of the time when you ask your friends and family members to criticise, there is a chance that they hesitate. Without criticism, you will not be able to grow, so it's vital to have someone who can do it for you.

• **New perspectives** -: when you are with the experienced person who had already travelled the path you are currently travelling then that person knows in which step you need to take more care.

He will help you to see your goal with a new perspective and mindset to approach your goal which you never be able to get if you don't have a mentor. If you take advice from the wrong person then he will give you the wrong perspective which will make it hard to achieve your goals.

- **Encouragement -:** When you have a mentor then you will feel more confident and secured in yourself because you know from inside that I am getting advice from a person who has already travelled this path. Sometimes you will feel low and unmotivated, at that time your mentor's encouraging words will help you to get the lost motivation and again you come to track. Even while facing a challenge you will do your best. If you don't have a mentor that you will feel so much stress and negative thoughts will start coming into your mind. As a result you might give up.
- **Networking -:** There might be a chance that your mentor introduced you to his friends or business circle and when you meet new professional people you will get new opportunities. There might be a chance that you get new business opportunities and all these ultimately help you to reach your goals. Without a mentor, these things are not possible.
- **Accountability -:** Without having a mentor there might be a probable chance that you will get distracted, but when you are with a mentor you need to work consistently as there is someone(mentor) who is watching you and tracking your progress. The problem with most people are that they are not able to maintain consistency, as a result, they do not get the desired result but having a mentor easily solve this problem.

Steps to find perfect mentor-:

1) Clarify your goals-: First, take a piece of paper and write down what you want to achieve. Suppose you want to build a multimillion-dollar company in the next five years, so ask yourself now how having a mentor is going to ease your path.

2) Find out experts –: You have already decided what you want, now it's time to find and meet people who have already achieved the goal that you have decided. Meet more as many people as possible in a decided time frame. Identify whom you admire and has qualities you wish to embody.

3) Understand their teaching style-: When you go out in search of a mentor, you need to find a person who is genuinely interested in sharing his wisdom, see how they teach you to try to find red flags like destructive criticism. After analysis, everything decides the right mentor.

4) Meet consistently -: When you get the right mentor, start taking advice and knowledge from him consistently. Don't forget to say thank you at the end and appreciate his effort. It takes 50 hours to consider them a trusted connection so meet him consistently.

XVIII
Habits

Our habit shapes our life far more than we probably realised. About 43% of our daily actions are not taken by our consciousness but by habits. Our life to a large extent is the sum of all habits (good or bad) which determine the quality of our life. It takes an average of 66 days to make a habit and set your action and behaviour on autopilot.

Your habits are going to determine whether you are going to become successful or not. If you have habits that are aligned to serve your goals then only you will be able to get what you want else you will fail.

But the problem with most of the people is that they have set their goal and their habits are not serving to it rather than it is creating destruction, as a result, most people are not able to reach their goals. To become successful, you need to first have a successful habit.

Example-: Let's say there are two students Rohan and Amit. Rohan is good at studies and always gets good mark while Amit is not good at studies and get low marks. What do you think what causing marks differences, the answer is Rohan have habits like daily revisions, studying for 3 hrs daily, practising questions etc. Here Rohan's habits serve him toward his goal, while Amit has no fixed study routine, he wastes so much time watching TV, gaming etc., here Amit have habits which do not serve his study goal and also distract him from his goal.

People do not understand that they can't become successful in just one night nor they can get failure in just one night. Success is a long term process. Yes, they can achieve it for just one day but can't get success. example – lottery.

But they need to fix their habits to make success an automatic process.

Habits are our brain's way of increasing its efficiency. Our brain turns daily repetitive actions and behaviours into habits so that we perform them automatically without putting in too much effort.

First, to condition yourself to make good habits, you need to take care of all the things that you give access to through all your five senses.

" Keep your thought positive because your thoughts become your word, keep your word positive because your word becomes your behaviour, keep your behaviour positive because your behaviour becomes your habit, keep your habits positive because your habits become your values, keep your values positive because your values become your Destiny"

-: Mahatma Gandhi

1) What kind of people do we hang out with. This will going to affect the quality of your thought. You need to ask yourself. Are you hanging out with looser or winners, are they have willing to grow in life and what they are doing to do that, does they have a good mindset, what type of talks you share because all these things are going to make an

impact on your thought process.

Example -: you can't quit smoking if your friends are smokers.

2) What kind of information do you consume -: Are you reading good books, consuming educational content or are you wasting your most of the time on films, web series and Netflix.

Your thought process is so much affected by the information you consume daily.

3) What kind of music do you listen to -: Music has so much impact on our brain and it changes our perception to view the world. Are you consistently listening to the music which empowers you and motivates you towards your goals or are you consistently listening to music that puts you down in a state of stress and a feeling of sadness?

How habit works

James clear author of " Atomic habit", one of the best books ever written on habit, explained that our habit has four components in it: a cue that triggers a craving, which motivates a response that provides a reward that satisfies the craving.

How to create a good habit

The 1st rule for cue -: make it obvious

The 2nd rule for craving:- make it attractive

The 3rd rule for response:-make it easy

The 4th rule for reward:- make it satisfying

How to break a bad habit

The inverse of 1st rule for cue-:make it invisible

The inverse of 2nd rule for craving -: make it unattractive

The inverse of 3rd rule for response -: make it difficult

The inverse of the 4th rule for reward -: make it less satisfying

1. **First rule for cue-**:Human brain build habits by noticing repeated cue and predicting outcomes without our consciousness being involved. Therefore awareness is the key to changing habits.

Habits scorecard is a good way of being aware of your good and bad habits. Make a list of your daily habits if it is a good habit, write "+" next to it, if it is a bad habit write "-" next to it and if it's a neutral habit write "="

Example-: Taking a shower daily +

Not drinking enough water –

Reading a book for 30 min +

Then use habit stacking means rather than pairing your new habit with a particular time and location, you can pair it with a current habit. This method will help you to make a cue for a new habit.

Example-: After taking my morning shower I will meditate for 10 minutes

After taking my morning coffee I will do a workout for 20 minutes.

Motivation is overvalued while the environment often matters more, you need to design your environment for success so that it favours your new habit. You need to make some changes in your environment so that you make things easy. Example -: If you want to make a habit of drinking water (3-4 litre) then you need to place a water bottle in the places where you spend your most time so that it will be easy to get without any effort. If you are trying to come out of the bad habit of drinking alcohol then stop its access, do not bring it home or place it in your fridge.

2. **The Second rule is to make it attractive-**: Habits are dopamine-driven feedback loops and when dopamine

rises so motivation also rises to perform that activity. Dopamine is released not only when you experience pleasure but also when you anticipate it.

Example -: Cocaine addicts get a surge of dopamine when they see the powder even before they take it.

We need to make our habit attractive because it is the expectation of a rewarding experience that motivates us to take the first action.

Temptation building can make your habits more attractive – It works on the principle of linking actions you want to do with actions you need to do. We tend to adopt habits that were praised by our culture because we have a strong desire to fit into it. So we tend to mimic the habits of three social groups:-

Close one's (friends and family)

A habit which follows by abundant people in our society

Habits of powerful people(status and money)

These behaviour get approval, respect and praise which make them attractive. One of the effective ways to build a better habit is to join a culture where your desire behaviour is normal behaviour

And you already have something in common.

Habit becomes attractive when it is associated with a positive feeling, so before going to the gym next time don't tell yourself " I am going to lift weights" but instead say " I am going to build a good physique".

3. **Third rule is to make it easy** -: The problem with most people is that they try to make a massive habit. Example -: reading a chapter every day, running 1 hr every day. But our brain does not want to come out of our comfort zone as a result we start procrastinating. You need to

trick your brain by taking small steps. Example-: reading 1 page every day, running for just 10minutes.

Most behaviour are governed by momentum, so you need to make momentum by taking small steps while starting any new habit. Forget about perfection just focus on repetition it's a key for habit formation.

4. **Fourth rule is to make it satisfying** -:The Cardinal rule of behaviour is simple. What is rewarded is repeated and what is punished is avoided. You need to decide rewards and punishments for good and bad behaviour.

If you miss one day then try to go back into it as quickly as possible.

Here are some habits of high achievers and successful people, try to adopt these habits to make significant changes in your life-:

1) **Taking 100% responsibility**:- Successful people always take full responsibility for their life. This habit gives them the power to take control of their life. They never complain, never blame others for their problems. They know that they have chosen their friends, with whom they spend time. By blaming others you give control of your life to the surrounding.

3) **Knowing their priorities** -: They are aware of what are the most important tasks to be done and they do them first. They do not want to waste their time, energy and effort on something less valuable. So they prioritize their task.

4) Having morning rituals-: They know that the key to starting the super productive day starts with a morning ritual. So they choose to make rituals that inspire and energize them.

5) Daily meditation or mindfulness technique -: Tim Ferriss author of the "4-hour workweek" discover from interviewing successful people that 80% of them practice some form of mindfulness in daily life like meditation and journaling.

6) Prioritize health -: Research has found that regular exercise and a healthy diet boost level of productivity, motivation and happiness.

7) Sharpening their skill -: They consistently work on their skills and knowledge and cultivate them. Bill gates read 50 books a year, Warren Buffet read almost 500 pages every day. They know the more they learn the more they earn. They try to make 1% improvement every day in their craft.

8) Taking a calculating risk

9) Optimistic -: They know the power of positivity and try to find positive things even in a negative situation of failure.

10) Having a goal and vision -: They know without goals in life, they will not be able to improve.

11) Surround with positivity-: They know the importance that to perform good they need to spend their time with positive, empowering and high achievers.

They know that they are the average of 5 people with whom they hang out the most.

12) Communicate effectively-: Our quality of life is determined by the quality of communication that we have with ourselves and the people around us.

They know the importance of clear communication in their career and relationships.

13) They are not afraid to fail and does not give up easily, they see failures as a learning process that helps them to grow.

14) They are proactive towards what they want in their life.

15) They practise gratitude -: They know without gratitude they can't feel more happiness and satisfaction for what they already have in their life.

16) Stable Emotion-: They know how to deal with emotions as life does not go smooth. Someday you win and someday you fail. They know how to handle their emotion in a tough time without losing hope.

17) Importance of smart work -: Smart work is finding a way to take maximum advantage of hard work.

XIX
Parenting

Parents are so much concerned about how to raise a child. For most of the parents, it's one of the difficult tasks as they don't know actually how to do parenting. Due to the wrong parenting technique, the relationship between parents and child suffers, the child becomes rebellious, angry, get into trauma. Most parents in our country do not know how to handle and discipline their children, as a result, they beat their children for small things. Parents are not aware that time has changed so much and they still apply the same parenting technique that they have learned from their parents which results in a problem between the relationship between the child and parents. Chanakya believes that parenting is the art of understanding child psychology. He had said that " For the first five years, the child should be given so much love and care. In this phase parents should not get angry even when his child makes a mistake. Parents should spend their time and should play with children. The child's brain is developing in this phase, they are observing and learning from the environment.

From age six to fifteen they should be disciplined as the capability of a child to think rationally starts developing, parents should guide their child to develop good healthy habits, their bad behaviour should be fixed. Developing discipline in a child does not mean that you are beating your child, you need to understand the psychology of your child.

Example – Let's say your child does not want to eat green vegetables, you should not force your child to eat vegetables rather than you can give your child an option to choose between two vegetables.

Yes, as a parent you should be strict with a child in some situations and the behaviour of your child. Examples-: you are not going to beat your younger sibling. You need to create boundaries that they are not going to cross, being strict to certain behaviours prevents the child to takes you for granted. Encourage them to read books, you as a parents should also read and both of you (child and parents) can discuss what they learn and understand from the book. Your child is not going to listen to you if you command them to read a book, they follow and learn from you, so when you engage yourself to read the book, your child is going to observe you and learn from you.

After sixteen years, the majority portion of your parenting is over now. Teach and guide your child to take responsibility for their life, tell them that you are not always going to be with them for a lifetime, so encourage them to make good decisions in their life, this will help your child to gain confidence.

Let them learn from their mistakes, teach them the cause and effect of their decision. Example- If they don't want to study for the exam and want to hang out with friends then tell them the consequences of the choice they will have in the future, especially if your child is a teenager, guide them but don't force them to make certain decisions, teach them to think in the long term in their life, teach them critical thinking skills and encourage their innovation, creativity, art and any skills that they have.

Teach them how to think, give them different perceptions to see things. The ultimate aim of parenting is to raise an independent, kind, capable individual, who can make their life decision of their own. Be his one of the close wise friend.

Types of parenting style-:

1) Democratic parenting style -: In this type of parenting style, parents encourage their child to achieve high in their lives but also have warmth towards their child. Parents are responsive and also have clear discipline rules and they should explain the reasons behind it and value boundaries with their children. In this parenting style, parents are supportive and value their independence. They involve their child in conversation and have frequent communication. These types of parents are nurturing.

As a result -: The child can achieve high in their academics, are more happy and independent, have more self-esteem, have better social skills, have less chance of getting into mental illness and depression, exhibits less violent tendencies and are more attached to their parents.

2) Authoritarian parenting style-: In this type of parenting style, parents are so strict and are controlling parents. These parents think that to set their children on the right path they need to be strict with them to discipline them. These parents are like a dictator, " If I told you to do it, you need to do it anyway". These parents are unresponsive to their child needs and desire and are not nurturing. They justify their harsh behaviour towards their child as a " tough love". These parents violate the boundaries of their children by checking their phones or reading personal diaries.

As a result -: The child is usually unhappy, have low self-esteem or self-worth, are usually less independent, appear insecure, have poor social skills, are more prone to getting into depression or suffering from mental illness, they are not able to establish boundaries with other relationship in their life, as a result, they suffer from trauma. These children get easily into addictions and are usually violent.

3) Permissive parenting style -: In this type of parenting style, parents do not have any boundaries and rules with their child. Whatever their child demands, these parents fulfil them.

These parents aren't able to say "NO" just because they do not want to disappoint their children. These parents are warm and indulgent. Example-: Suppose your child demanded you a new phone, you as a parent give it to him immediately without thinking about it much.

As a result -: The Child doesn't follow any rules, have poor self-control, always try to seek out instant gratification, have low self-esteem, poor social skills, as they do not know about setting boundaries they usually make the relationship in their life toxic for others and possess egocentric behaviour.

4) Neglectful parenting style-: In this type of parenting style parents are cold and unresponsive. These parents hardly care about what their child needs and desire. They don't set any boundaries. These types of parents might be suffering from depression or any other mental illnesses, might get abused or neglected when they were children. They hardly care with whom their child is hanging out either it is good or bad company.

As a result -: The child gets into addictive behaviour of drugs and alcohol, lack self-control, has low self-esteem, usually suffering from mental illness, are more prone to suicidal thought, getting into depression and displays violent and impulsive behaviours.

In all these four parenting styles, The Democratic style is a good choice for parents for raising a happy, independent and successful individual and all other three are usually a toxic style of parenting.

Sign of toxic parents -:

• **Controlling parents** – (one of the most common and toxic parenting styles of our country) -: If you as a parents choose the wrong parenting style then there is a major probability of developing a toxic relationship with your child. Many parents especially in our country thinks that their child will not become successful or achieve anything in their life if they do not follow the path that they have dictated, and start controlling everything in the life of their child without listening to the wants and desires of their child and starts micromanaging the life of their child. When parents start controlling the life of their child, constantly try to manipulate and control the decision, feeling and action, they start dictating what colleges you should go to and what career and path you should choose even it goes against your desire. Because of these, things becomes so toxic. Even when children grow up and become adults, these parents are dictating whom you should marry.

When a child is raised in this way they are not able to develop the confidence and self-esteem that they needed to achieve and succeed in their life. Parents now a day become so much obsessed and over concerned whether their child is getting a top score in class or not, whether they are getting awards or not , as by this they measure the worth of their child. They want their child to be so much perfect. Many parents think that their child has no future if they do not follow the career, college that they chose for them. Most parents are obsessed to send their children to Harvard and Stanford. In our country - IIT colleges if he belongs to the maths field and MBBS colleges if he belongs to biology. You have to be an engineer, doctor, CA, IAS, IFS etc. you only have these selective choices for a career in our country.

If you as parents dare to look at the scenario, you will see that majority of the time you have some type of ego attached to certain colleges and career paths, so to fulfil their fantasy they are obsessed with it.

Many parents want to brag about the college they have sent their child, to their friends and neighbours to feel superior. You think that your child will not have any future if they don't go to these selective colleges but that is not the actual reality. If you look around yourself and see the top 10% of wealthy people around yourself you will easily get the answer, the majority of them are not from these top college but are wealthy, happy and successful. If you think that your child will not be able to earn money from the career path they have chosen, then you are thinking wrong. In modern time, in every domain(career) there are so many opportunities that have arisen due to the Internet. There is no skill in the market in this internet era that can't be capitalised.

There will be more opportunities in the upcoming decade, so don't pressurize your child to make choices between some selective career, listen to your child about what he/ she is interested in and support him.

If you are a controlling parent then you are subconsciously rewiring your child mind to think that they are not capable enough to make their own decisions and choices in their life. As a result, they are not able to get confidence in themselves. As a result, when your child will become an adult he/she will become dependent, due to lack of confidence they will not be able to achieve greater heights in their life as he/she had never done it before by themselves. Controlling behaviours of the parent restrict the child to think that their parents action led to the outcome and not their own actions

This will help your child to think a lot, discloses, plan, trial and error, dreaming, experiencing their life and all these will only happen when you encourage them to make a decision and take responsibility for their life. Rather than being over-concerned about college or career path you as parents should be more concerned about your child having a good successful habit, do they have the right mindset to achieve success, do they have a growth mindset, do they have a good work ethic, do they have critical thinking skill and problem-solving skill, do they have kindness, financial knowledge, do they have a bounce-back attitude after getting a failure, do they have a willingness to contribute to society and make a positive impact on mankind. These are the most important factors you need to be concerned about.

If your child has these traits no matter what career field he/ she chooses they will be able to achieve high in that field. You need to understand and accept the harsh reality that – the child comes through you this does not mean that you have the right to control and dictate his/ her life.

" It's not your child, almost you are just given a genetic substance to create a body, you can't create a life don't have a grandiose idea about yourself" – Sadhguru

There is a major chance that your child will get into a trauma state when you as parents have controlling behaviour. It lowers the happiness index of a child, kills his creativity and innovation.

Can you imagine if your child has a desire to become a singer and you are constantly manipulating him and affecting him that he is wasting time and there is no career in it, this will directly affect the mental health of your child until your child already possess a strong belief in his own abilities?

If you are reading this chapter and facing this problem as there might be chance your parents have a rigid thought process then you need to leave that environment as much fast as possible else you will get into a trauma state and feel frustrated and might get into depression. You need to accept the fact that you can't change your parents nor it's your job to fix their thought processes. Maybe in future, they will change their mindset but for now take control of your own life, leave the toxic environment if you want to rise in life and to feel happy and satisfied.

- **Invasive parents** -: when parents do not have any boundaries or constantly violate the boundaries of their child, they check your phone without permission, read your diary etc. Here, when the boundaries of your child are constantly violated then it will create trust issue and the child starts hiding things from you, become rude and lose emotional connection with you. Parents need to teach their children that " boundaries are important to establish healthy relationships with anyone", many adults now a day face so many problems in relationships with their partners just because they have not learned how to set healthy boundaries, As a result, they suffer in a relationship and gets into a traumatic state.

If your child is a teenager don't violate their boundaries. You as parents can set boundaries for their screen time, sleep time, make a rule about their homework and studies.

Setting boundaries in parenting depends on the age of your child if he is small (10 years old) their boundaries and rules should be different from a child (17-year-old), maybe the younger child will be more restricted to certain things.

• **Verbal abusive parent:** Yes, there are parents in our country who verbally abuse their child in some ways. When they constantly affirm to their child that he/ she is a useless person then it starts affecting the self-worth and self-esteem of the child. They lose confidence and stats seeing themselves as looser. This happens because the child's brain is developing and his believes have not become strong, so they start getting affected by verbal abuse. This is one of the destructive forms of communication. It becomes worse when parents start verbally abusing their children in public. In this state, the child loses his self-esteem and gets into a traumatic state.

If you want to criticise your child then practice "constructive criticism", set boundaries with a child that you are not going to verbally abuse them. You need to accept the fact that if your child has poor social skills, is unstable, argumentative, rigid, undisciplined, rude, anti-social behaviour, have a fear of failure, having a problem with setting boundaries, careless, these all happened because of bad parenting.

Parenting tips for parents to raise happy, satisfied and successful individuals:-

• Read books, listen to the podcast and watch the educational inspiring video along with your child. Don't just tell them to do it alone because your child does not listen to your word but will follow you. So you need to involve with him and after completion of the book/ video/ podcast ask questions and share your perspective.

- Teach your child about finances, give them some money every week and teach them budgeting. Budgeting will help your child to practice delayed gratification. As when your child has a desire to buy a video game then he has to wait for a certain period to get it.
- Encourage questioning and writing -: when he starts questioning about things and gets deeper into finding why and how then he will gradually develop critical thinking skills. When he write and ask the right questions. Give him a scenario and perspective and ask questions about it.
- Encourage your child learning and speaking skill. When your child learns then he will become innovative and gets more idea. When they learn speaking skill then they can express their opinions to a large group of people, this will help them to develop confidence.
- Encourage his talent and skills, make them join the course to improve and refine their skills. If they are passionate about singing then make them join the singing course, if he is interested in football then let him join football training.
- Embrace Little struggle, failure and risk. This will help your child to become more emotionally strong and also help them to develop can-do and bounce-back attitudes.
- Tell him stories of growth mindset, discipline stories, watch documentaries with them some time.
- Many parents in our country put rigid though about caste and religion in their child minds.

As a result, children are subconsciously making some form of discrimination and start to think that their religion, colour and caste are more superior compared to others. Don't be this kind of parent, raise your child without putting any ill-thought about skin colour, caste and religion. Also, teach them gender equality.

- Teach your child about appropriate and inappropriate touches(sexual touches), and also tell them to tell you whenever someone touches them inappropriately.
- We are living in an era of the internet and a major portion of the Internet contains porn and sexually explicit content, so as parents you need to give them sex education, also guide them on how they are going to handle sexual content.
- In the last decades, social media become so much common and there is a mass bulk of content uploaded every day. you as a parent need to set some boundaries about the content that your child should watch. You should tell them how this crap content and their devices are destroying or can destroy their life, how their studies, productivity, focus, social skill are affected by it.

You need to understand that the content your child is watching is rewiring your child mind. So if he/she start and end his day with Instagram reels and consuming other waste content then you need to fix their screen time.

- You as a parents need to avoid your screen time to some extent, as the child is learning from you, so before making your child disciplined you first need to make yourself disciplined. How can you expect your child to wake up at 6 AM if you wake up at 8 AM?
- Parents should involve in some form of donations to charity. As you are setting a positive example there is a major chance that when your child becomes an adult he /she will also involve in charity.
- Admit to your child that you just landed on earth a few years before them, so they also do not know everything. You are also learning and experiencing new things in life. But yes you have more experience than them.

- The major problem with parents in our country is that parents compare grades, career, skills of their child with their neighbour's child or their friend's child. As a result child lose his unique potential and the child feels extra pressure from it. As a parent, you need to understand that every child is different and have different talent and skill, comparing your child is only going to lower your child self-worth.

- It's very vital to find time for yourself, things are going to be tough when both of you and your partner are working. But you and your partner have learn to balance the load of parenting, it's not just the work of one person. When you set boundaries and create the balance you will be able to make time, you might feel guilty while setting boundaries with the child but it will going to help you to live a life of less stress. It's okay to not be able to spend time every day with your child.

XX
Food habits

Most people in our society are not aware of the foods that they are putting into their bodies. Some people who know something about it also ignore it and get trapped into bad food habits. Remember knowing is not enough, you need to execute. In our generation, junk food is usually common and because of this many of us do not live longer, suffer from many diseases from an early stage. Already, the lifestyle of peoples are worse and we commonly face stress every day in some form, in addition to that, our food habit makes things much worse. Everyone wants to achieve high or wants to reach the goals of their life. While chasing their dream people do not take their health seriously, as a result even if they reach their goals they are not able to enjoy their life because of poor health. Remember that our body is a biological system, which requires certain types of food to function properly, you can't expect the good condition of the system(body) if you constantly eat crap. A major part of your health lies in the food habit that you are following. You can easily fight many diseases just by making positive changes in your food choices.

Including food choices, you need to understand that our body is designed for doing physical activity, but today's lifestyle usually does not involve any physical activity as we just sit in a chair most of the time. But if your physical activity is very low then how can you expect that your body is going to last longer.

Ayurveda advice on food choices

Ayurveda puts great stress on the food choices, what foods should be eaten and what should be avoided, when should be eaten and how should be eaten. You need to understand that even eating healthy food can also causes disease if we don't take them at proper timing. It will result in the accumulation of toxins in the body which further cause health issues.

First, you need to know about the timing of sunrise and sunset in whatever location you are living and according to that you are going to adjust your food habit. According to Ayurveda, digestive fire rises when the sun rises and gets at its peak when the sun is at its peak and gradually slow down when sun sets, so it's recommended to avoid food after sunset as food eaten after sunset is not properly digested in the body which result in the accumulation of toxins, but usually, this is not possible for many people, so for them it's advisable to take light food at night. Certain food like banana, radish, cucumber and curd should be prohibited as these food are extremely cold foods and our body will not be able to digest them properly at night. It's better to do intermittent fasting at night.

What should be eaten? Is one of the most common questions

According to Ayurveda food that is Saatvik, seasonal, local and tasty.

- Sattvic foods -: Ayurveda have divided food into three categories based on the nutritious value it contains. These foods make your mind clear, set you in a peaceful state. These are-:

1) Sattvic food-: Those foods which are full of goodness come into this category. This includes vegetarian foods such as green vegetables, fruits, cereals, seeds and legumes. It also includes fresh desi cow products.

2) Rajasic food -: These foods make your mind and body restless, make you aggressive and increase anxiety. It includes refined white sugar, coffee, onions and garlic, heavenly spicy food. Remember Even sattvik food transform into rajasic when prepared with so many spices.

3) Tamasic food-: These foods deplete your energy and make your mind dumb. These food are not good for you, this food can cause health issues when consumed consistently. These include frozen food, packed foods, all junk foods, preservative food, including non-veg.

- Seasonal foods -: Fruit and vegetables should be taken when they are in season. When you eat foods that are not in season then you are more prone to disease as they are stored in cold storage. You will not get the maximum benefit from it and also they will going to cost more money.

- Local food -: According to Ayurveda foods should be taken which are produced within a radius of 100 km. Usually, local foods are fresh foods. Food that is put into cold storage and transported lost their nutritious value and are unfresh.

Tasty food -: If your food is not giving you a good taste then you will not be able to force yourself to eat it over long period and end up getting back to junk foods. So it's important to learn new recipes so that you don't lose interest in eating healthy food. Don't eat the same type of food regularly, you need to make changes in food choices and for that you need to learn more recipes for sattvic foods.

Water -: Do not start to drink suddenly 3-4 litres of water from day one, improve your water intake gradually it will not overload your kidneys.

First, in the morning try to drink much water as possible according to your stomach and then after 30-60 minutes go to become fresh. If possible, try to place water in copper utensils or clay pot the night before going to sleep.

Many people believe that sattvic foods are not enough for protein sources, but that is not correct. If you properly manage your sattvik food then you will be able to get protein. We all know great martial artist Bruce Lee was vegetarian, so you can say a good body can be made with a vegetarian diet. Even today so many bodybuilders and sports personalities are maintaining training their bodies just following a vegetarian diet.

But at the end of the day, it's your choice to choose food. In western countries many people are suffering from Cancer compare to our country because their diet contains very high protein.

Consuming non-veg foods make you more prone to cancer as our body is not designed for eating flesh.

Brain foods

- Our body is the reflection of the food we intake consistently. Food has a great impact on our brain example – If you have anxiety disorder then you need to cut down your intake of coffee as it enhances restlessness. Our brain is mainly made up of fats, protein, amino acids, glucose etc. Each component has a direct impact on our mood, energy, happiness index, anxiety. So it is important that we give our brain, a certain type of food for its proper functioning and to get maximum benefits from it. If you do not then you will be more prone to mental health issues such as Alzheimer's, Parkinson's disease. Students should include brain foods in their diets as they boost cognitive function, memory power, thinking skills. There are some food mentioned below which are great for our brain -:

1) Omega 3 fatty acids -: It is vital for the normal functioning of the brain, lack of it accelerates the ageing process of the brain. Taken regularly in diet will improve memory power and cognitive function, helps you to fight against depression and other mental health problems. Very rich sources of omega 3 fatty acids are found in seafood (salmon fish, oysters, cod liver oil) but as we are following a vegetarian diet, so we need to consume seeds like -: flax seeds, chia seeds, sunflower seeds, pumpkin seeds, sesame seeds, walnuts, soybean. Mainstream health organizations recommend 250-500 mg of omega 3 for a normal adult, so you can easily get it from seeds. For your convenience, you can mix and grind all seeds together and take it first in the morning.

2) Berries-: Including blueberries, strawberries, blackberries, mulberry in your diet will help to protect you from Alzheimer's, Parkinson's disease and lower your blood pressure, also they are a great source of antioxidants. Berries are great for your skin healthy, helps you to look younger and slow down ageing.

3) Coffee-: Ayurveda doesn't recommend more than one cup of coffee in a day. As it comes under rajasic food type. But just taking one cup of coffee helps you to improve your mood, alertness, physical and mental performance.

It is a great source of antioxidant and help in fighting against Parkinson's disease, reduce the risk of cancer, strokes and also help in fat loss.

4) Oatmeal -: When it comes to carbohydrates, we should not forget about oats. If you intake mainly simple carbohydrates then it will cause high insulin, causing blood pressure issues and heart disease. So we all must include an oatmeal minimum of once a day, it's a great source of complex carbs which digest slowly and give energy consistently. Oats also contain a good source of fibres that helps in maintaining good digestion.

5) Turmeric -: This is one of the most common ingredients that we use on daily basis especially in our country. But we are not aware of the benefits that we are getting from it. Turmeric is rich in antioxidants and has an anti-inflammatory characteristic that boosts the immune system, turmeric contains curcumin which boosts the brain boosts drives neurotrophic factor (BDNF) which is further linked to improving brain function and lower the risk of heart disease.

6) Fresh green vegetables-: Vegetables like spinach, broccoli, beetroot, carrots, tomato etc are rich sources of vitamins and minerals such as zinc, potassium, vitamin – c, which help in slow down cognitive decline, better memory and thinking skill compared to those who don't consume them regularly. So it's vital to include salads in your diet, you can also make a smoothie by blending and start the day with it.

You should also include dark chocolate, coconut water and oil, bananas, sweet potatoes, oranges etc.

XXI
Boundary setting

Many people are not aware of boundaries to maintain healthy relationships. Due to a lack of boundaries setting many people gets into a trauma state and feel low self-esteem, low self-worth, guilt etc. The major problem is that people don't know about it, very few people especially in our country, know the importance of boundaries in relationships.

Let's first know what boundaries mean- boundaries are the limit that we set for ourselves that we will and will not tolerate. Suppose you and your friends are talking, one of your friends commented about one of your insecurity or any personal stuff and the whole group starts laughing and that comment made you feel bad. Here your friends have unconsciously violated your boundaries, as a result, you get into a trauma state. Now you have two options – 1) either ignore and start talking about a different topic 2) you can kindly express your feeling and tell your friends that I don't feel good so try not to talk about this thing else our friendship will suffer and may end in future. When you choose the first option then you will get trapped into guilt, low self-esteem and other bad emotions, also there is a major chance that your friends in the future will continue to violate your boundaries. If you choose the second option then you reinforce boundaries to some topics if you have a good friend then they will respect your boundaries else you have an option to leave them. But the problem with the majority populations is that they choose the first option and do not communicate their boundaries.

You need to understand one thing that we live in the 21st century and if you become kind to people without setting any boundaries and try to over help, or take over responsibility then you will be going to suffer in some way. In the end, you will only get the feeling of a loser even after putting your lot of effort(time, energy, money) to fix other person's problems or trying to make them happy. The problem with many people is that they have a behaviour of people-pleasing, to make other people feel good they start to prioritizing other people first which is not a good thing. There can be so many reasons that you have a habit of people-pleasing or putting other people's first while neglecting your own needs, your childhood programming can be one of the causes that you have this behaviour in your personality. Suppose one of your parent(father) have a habit of drinking alcohol and when your teenage year starts and at that time your alcoholic parent gets into ill health and doctor advice him not to do any work and take rest. Due to this, you grow in an environment where you have to do so many works including taking family responsibility from a very early age, and over the period, you start prioritising your ill father needs, happiness first and start putting your happiness, your goals and dreams second. After a few years, your father dies but your behaviour of putting others first will not go. This is just one cause, there are many other causes too.

Suppose you were raised in an environment where your parents constantly violate your boundaries(could be anything from reading your diary or reading your chats) as a result you are not able to know that things like boundaries also exist in relationships. Maybe your parents always tell you to be a nice person, avoid conflicts, as a result, it gives birth to self-sacrificing behaviour in you. That behaviour is left into your personality, as a result – you don't have your own opinion, you aren't able to present your opinions just to avoid any conflict or maybe you don't want to hurt another person. You need to understand one thing that there is a difference between being kind and being nice to someone. Kindness comes with boundaries. You need to understand that no matter what a nice person does people are not going to respect him/ her and in addition to that people will take advantage of you.

There is a huge difference between how a nice person sees himself and other people see him.

Suppose you are a nice person then you will think that -: I am helping every person who comes to me, I don't say "NO" to anyone so that another person does not feel bad or get hurt, I am always there for my friends and family every time they asked me, I had sacrificed my needs to make them happy. So why do these people don't respect me, ignore me and my needs and don't care about me. This means that all these people are bad and take advantage of me. This is how a nice person sees himself. Other people see and think that – he does not have any opinions of himself, he is always available whenever I want him, he has prioritised others happiness and takes the responsibility for others without doing something good for himself and he is not doing anything in his life, maybe he doesn't have any goals so I can assume that he will struggle and his future in darkness, he doesn't have anything to do so he is always available. This is how other peoples see the nice person. So being a nice person is not a good thing, so if you have this mindset then change it. A simple definition of a nice person is someone who does not have any boundaries.

If I tell you not to be a nice person, then it does not mean that I am telling you to become an asshole person(who become jealous of others, try to take advantage of others, try to harm others in some ways), what I am telling you is to become a self-respecting guy, who inspires respect from another person, a person who is genuinely admired by others.

Now let's see how to set healthy boundaries and avoid being a nice person -:

• First, you need to introspect and analyse your life situations and see what are the things that make you feel bad around people.

• You need to directly communicate with people that these are my limits or tolerance level. Example-: suppose your friend comes to your house for a few days then you can clearly say to him that you can't smoke in my house, you can't use my clothes etc. When people are aware that these are the limits then they will not violate them.

You need to have some values and standards for yourself, below that you will not going to accept. When you set boundaries you might lose some people but you need to understand that these are toxic people and are not good for you, they are manipulators. Good people will always respect your boundaries.

• Stop prioritizing other people happiness, their life over yours. Learn to say "NO". Many people have the misconception that saying 'No' is rude but that's not true.

You can say no in a rude way or you can say no kindly.

• Remember "NO" is a complete sentence, sometimes you don't have to give a reason. But if you want to you can. Example-: sorry I will not be able to come to your birthday party because I have some important office work.

• Don't allow other people to emotionally manipulate you and make you feel guilty for saying "NO". Remember so many people will try to manipulate you.

• Say to yourself that -: I don't want to be liked by everyone, I want respect and to get the respect I need to stand for myself, my opinion, for my goals and dream, my happiness. Even if people don't like me.

• You need to make a priority list and before helping others you need to first help yourself. Make your career, finances, goals, happiness, hobbies, things that you like doing etc your top priority especially if you are in your early twenties, if you are prioritizing anything other than that then it will be your biggest mistake.

If you waste your time, energy and money to help others, after 5-10 years you will realise that you have fucked up your life helping people who don't respect and value you.

If you constantly support someone and work for someone's life then what about your dreams and goals.

• Remember the rule before wasting time on helping others or taking extra- responsibility – first, let me fix my life, let me first fulfil my responsibility for myself and my future, let me first work on my happiness index. Then only I can help you.

• Stop being always available for others rather than get busy working on your goals and dream list. People will not respect you if you are not taking action towards creating a better life.

- Stop taking over-responsibility, we spend a lot of energy caring about the perceptions of other people emotions and how they see you. As a result, you put other emotions first and ignore your inner voice, stop doing this.
- You should not care about other people emotions (sad, anger etc) after expressing your true self, it's their responsibility to deal with them as it's their emotions. You need to focus on putting yourselves and your needs first.
- Stop trying to over-explain to yourself why I said No, initially when you start setting boundaries you might feel uncomfortable and sad but remember that's good for you. Over some time and practice, you will feel normal after saying "No".
- Everyone is doing what is best for themselves and their life and if you are just helping and doing the best for others, not for yourself then no one will going to respect you and look after you. Remember " Before making a Palace for others first make it for yourself".
- Never change yourself and ignore your own needs to please someone else. Be authentic and express yourself.

Don't let anyone even your family members, parents, partner, friends to violate your boundaries.

- Even if you have any type of family issue (could be the death of parents, ill family members, fight between parents or any type of problem) as a result you are taking over-responsibility then you need to manage the problem that you are facing so that it doesn't hamper your dream or long term goal.

XXII
Critical thinking

We live in a world where we are consistently bombarded by many decisions every day, it is impossible to make the perfect decision. Critical Thinking is one of the most important cognitive skills that you can develop. By improving the quality of both decisions and your thought, it improves your life both professionally and personally.

It is key to career growth. There are many professions where critical thinking is an absolute must. Lawyers, doctors, accountants, engineers and scientists and many others frequently apply this skill.

Critical Thinking is one of the ways which can help us make a perfect decision in those particular situations. It is important because we are bombarded with advertisements, facts, people around us which influence our decision if we do not think critically. It teaches the best way to evaluate evidence and using the result to come up with new innovative new solutions to the problems.

Critical Thinking is the intellectually disciplined process of actively and skilfully conceptualizing, applying, synthesizing and evaluating information gathered from observations, experience, reflection, reasoning to make a good solution for a problem. Critical Thinking allows us to carefully deconstruct the situation, reveal hidden issues like manipulation and bias and make us aware of the problem which helps us to make the best decision.

If you are not thinking critically then you are relying on emotion, people, feeling, memory, facts from the society to think and make a decision which is the worst thing which you can do in this modern world. Instead of taking ideas, beliefs, facts from society start analysing them and thinking about them. Critical Thinking can make you happier, we all know that the quality of our life is mostly depends upon the quality of decisions.

It is an excellent tool to help you to understand yourself better and to learn to master your thoughts. You can use critical thinking to free yourself from cognitive biases, negative thinking and limiting beliefs that hold you back from a completely different life. It helps you to access your strengths and weaknesses so that you can work on them and improve. Critical thinking improve relationships, it makes you more open-minded which helps you to understand others point of view. You can detect when others are being disingenuous, trying to take advantage or manipulates you.

Before we learn about " critical thinking " we need to follow some key rules-:

- You will not use emotion, feelings, memory(good or bad) bias to reach any decision, just forget your emotions.
- Critical Thinking needs curiosity, analysis, logic, creativity and rational thinking.
- You need to be an independent thinker and open-minded and also stop thinking in binary. Thinking in binary means – you have only two options such as black or

white, good or bad etc.

Steps of critical thinking

1) Understand the Information -: First organise the information, fact and data. Understand the main ideas and also summarise it, explore their boundaries.

2) Understand the information with others views, try to see with other perceptions. You can assume that you are a scientist living on the moon and with his telescope, you are watching and studying the life of a person, any situation of a person living on earth and being a third party you give advice.

3) Asking the right question -: Critical thinking is all about asking the right questions, it involves stepping back to view all angles and perceptions to make the right decision. For example: when someone tells you something, before you rush to judgment, try to formulate a response stop and ask questions.

You need to ask questions like-:

a) Who said it? -: From where do you get the information, facts and data.

b) Why did they say it?/ what is the information?/ what is the problem?

c) Why the problem arises, it's cause and effect.

-: Most of the time we need to go with a series of "why" to get the root cause of the problem.

d) How to solve this problem?

4) Find Errors in your thinking -: sometimes our brain gives solutions based on our pre-existing beliefs and use

Conclusion to justify the proof.

Write- writing helps us to organize our thoughts and make us aware of the problem.

"The best way to teach people critical thinking is to teach them to write"- Jordan Peterson

Great writers are great thinkers. To write well is to think that's why it is so hard but writing exercises our thinking ability. Great writing requires observation, reflection, evaluation and artful representation of information. By improving your writing you can improve thinking skill. Writing all improve conceptual learning, studies have found that the " reflective nature of writing process contributes to effective learning".

World most top universities like Harvard, Stanford etc takes essay tests while taking admission just to check their(grammar and critical thinking skill). Reasons why essay writing improves critical thinking -:

1. Inspecting the reliability of information – while writing essays students have to evaluate the reliability of data that they have. Where did it come from and how it was acquired? Does it serve something and is there any reason to assume it could be biased and manipulated.

2. Differentiating facts and opinions-: Evaluating different sources of data is important when presenting an argument. There is a difference between backing up your argument with facts and opinions. Students will learn that facts are truths and they can be proven while opinions are only based upon an experience, feelings and beliefs which can't be examined.

3. Reflecting on information -: Writing an essay allows students to understand how they react to information. Do they agree or disagree with it. Does it make them feel surprised, excited or confused?. And most important why they react that way.

4. Making decisions -: Decision making is a crucial part of critical thinking. It concern how we make the most optimal choice between different possibilities. Students need to make decisions when they are writing an essay and have to choose the best way to make an argument.

5. Using the information in different forms -: Understanding how information is presented is essential for formatting arguments. Students will learn how to use data in different forms. Examples- graph, table and charts etc.

6. Analysing argument -: Before a student can draw their conclusions, they must evaluate arguments from other people. Does the argument make sense in light of all evidence? While formulating their thoughts in essay, students will have to evaluate existing arguments. Can they find flaws in it and is there a way to improve or use creativity to fix problems.

7. Presenting arguments-: Writing an essay is a good way to learn how to present their argument after forming judgements and making their decision. It helps them to communicate more effectively along with thinking clearly.

To think critically, you need to be aware of cognitive biases which impact our thinking and decision-making skill.

Let's see what is cognitive bias and how it affects it?

Cognitive bias is a systematic error in thinking that occurs when people are processing and interpreting information in the world around them which affect the decision and judgment that they make. Cognitive biases are often a result of our brain attempts to simplify information processing and how our emotional response to situations and people. Some of these are related to memories- the way we remember events and others are related to a problem in attention while receiving the information. It leads to distorted thinking.

All critical thinker rigorously questions ideas and assumptions rather than accepting any beliefs and thoughts. The ability to think critically does not come naturally to most people. It is a skill that takes time and effort to develop. But being able to think critically plays a huge role in how successful you are in life. Without it, you might miss so many good decisions in your life, and these decisions automatically affect the quality of your life.

Factors that contribute to these biases are -: Emotions, the limit of our mind's ability to process information, social pressure, the influence of people around us, individual motivation etc. Our brain plays tricks on us - the mind usually likes to take shortcuts, our brain usually become lazy when trying to solve a new problem or making a new decision, so our mind often falls back on the rules of solution that have worked well in the past and usually does not stress to think from starting(new perspective). While making a decision or judgement, you like to think that you are logical, rational, analytical and capable of making decisions after evaluating the information that is available to you. But sadly that does not happen most of the time, these biases unconsciously affect the thinking which leads to poor decisions. So we need to become aware of it so that we can reduce them.

The reality is that no one is capable of removing all the biases but we can reduce them so that we can make good decisions and judgement.

Remember that cognitive biases are not necessarily all bad, because many of these biases help us in adaptation and survival purposes. They all help us to reach a decision quickly, this can be vital if you are facing a dangerous or threatening situation. Example- suppose you are going back to home from the office and due to office work you are late, while going you notice that few unknown peoples are following you from their vehicles. At this moment, your brain starts to think – and comes to a conclusion that these people can be kidnappers or muggers and you are in danger as your brain already had data for these types of situations from news, friends, family etc, so you start driving fast and come out of this danger.

Here relying on mental shortcut helped you to come out of the threatening situation.

Many peoples confuse between logical fallacy and cognitive biases-: Logical fallacy occurs when there is an error in a logical argument while cognitive biases are related to thought processing errors that often arises from a problem with attention, emotions, memory and other mental mistakes.

Now we are going to briefly discuss some of these common biases related to day to day life. So that you can have a basic idea about them.

1) Anchoring bias -: It occurs when people rely too much on the first information or pre-existing information while making a decision.

Example-: Suppose you have gone to buy a shirt if you see first shirt cost rupees 2500 – then sees a second shirt cost rupees 2000 then you will be likely to see the second shirt as cheap. Whereas if you only have seen the second shirt's price rupees 2000 you'd probably not view it as cheap.

So here the first price that you saw unconsciously influences your opinion.

Usually, this bias is so much used in sales and marketing, first sellers show you the high priced product then they lower the price or show you moderate price products.

2) Confirmation bias-: It is a type of bias that involves favouring or actively searching for the information that confirms your pre-existing beliefs or ideas. Confirmation bias impact how we gather information and also they influence how we recall and interpret them.

Example-: suppose you support a particular issue in that case, you will try to seek more information to support it, you might create new stories to supports it and going to ignore the information that opposes it.

3) Backfire effect-: Some people tend to resist accepting the evidence(information) that conflicts with their beliefs. It is a subtype of confirmation bias, showing people evidence that proves that they were wrong is often ineffective and causes them to backfire by causing them to support their original belief more strongly than they previously did.

Example-: Introducing peoples to negative information about a person whom they like often cause them to increase in liking for that person, this usually happens to some people.

4) Framing effect-: It occurs when our decision is influenced by the way information is presented.

Example -: suppose Rohit is gone to buy a floor cleaner, in the shop he saw two different brands of a cleaner of the same price . The first cleaner claims to kill 95% of germs while the second cleaner claims that only 5% germs will survive.

After comparing Rohit buy the first one as he didn't like the sound germ surviving. Here the way information is being presented impacts the opinion.

5) In-group bias-: It is the tendency of people to be more helpful and positive towards the members of their group over members of out-groups.

Example-:group of religious beliefs, political ideologies, same occupation, cultural group etc.

6) Barnum effect-: It refers to our tendency to think that the information provided about our personalities is about us regardless of how much it is generalized. It occurs when an individual believes that the personality description applies specifically to him even though the description is applied to many peoples. Because of this, peoples are so much interested in reading their horoscope or beliefs in personality tests.

7) Dunning-Kruger effect-: In this type of bias, people thinks that they are smarter, intellectual and capable than they are. This happens because of low self-awareness. These people fail to recognize their own mistakes and lack skill and knowledge.

Example -: At school/ college, this bias can make it difficult for students to recognize and correct their poor performance. This same applies to workplaces where people don't recognize their poor performance.

8) Fundamental attribution error -: In this type of bias people tend to assume another person that their actions depend on what kind of person that person is rather than on social and environmental factors that include that person.

Because of this, we tend to think that people do bad things because they are a bad person, here we ignore the social factor that influences another person's decisions or actions.

Example -: While driving, if someone is cut off you might think that " he is a jerk" instead of ignoring the possibility that they might be late for their office or they are rushing to drop someone at the airport. On the flip side when we cut someone off in traffic then we convince ourselves that we are late for the office, here we focus much on the situation rather than our character for that behaviour.

9) Placebo effect-: Phenomenon in which a fake treatment inactive substance like sugar pills/ saline solutions can sometimes improve the patient's condition, just because they are expecting that it will work. Here patient beliefs in medicine and treatment psychologically impact him and convince him that he is healing from it.

This tells us that our brain plays a major role in healing any type of physical or mental health issue.

10) Halo effect -: The tendency for positive/ negative impression of person/ company/ product or brand in one area to positively/ negatively influence one's feelings or opinions in other areas.

Example- A good looking person in front of them is also an intellectual, polite person. But in reality, there is no relation between his/ her good looks with his/ her politeness but our brain usually inter-link them.

11) Bystander effect-: It refers to a phenomenon in which the greater number of people are present, the less likely people are going to help a person in distress. In an emergency, the observer is more likely to help the distressed person when there is little or no one witnesses. This happens because in the group as other observers are also present causes the – diffusion of responsibility, observers do not feel pressure and as a result, they don't take action and wait for others to take responsibility. For Example- suppose whenever there is a fight going on the road then a crowd of people usually stop and watches rather than taking action to resolve the fight.

12) Availability -bias -: Tendency of people to use information that comes into their mind easily and quickly while making decisions and judgments about the future. It happens because of a mental shortcut that relies on immediate examples.

Example-: when a person consume news about child trafficking frequently then your mind convinces you to believe that this thing has become much more common than they truly are.

13) Belief bias -: When the conclusion supports your existing beliefs then you will rationalize anything that supports it. This happens when individual own values, beliefs, knowledge distorts the reasoning process through the acceptance of invalid arguments or data.

Example-: suppose you like a person then you start giving useless and invalid reasons for why you like them, irrespective of concluding and analysing the real data about them.

14) Bandwagon effect-: It is a type of group thinking, which make us believe in something because other peoples also believe in it. Because of this bias, person puts it's individual belief, behaviour, style aside and follow what other people's believes, behaviour and style belonging to that group. It's a herd mentality that can negatively impact society sometimes when people in a group hold negative or wrong beliefs about health, gender, race etc.

15) Optimism bias-: it's a bias that makes us feel that the chance of experiencing a positive event is higher and the chance of experiencing a negative event is lower in the path of achieving something.

16) Negativity bias-: Due to this bias we tend to focus and exaggerate in our mind so much on small negative things or event happens to us and while ignoring all the good things which had also happened. Which causes stress, anxiety, low self-esteem, which affect our health.

17) Self-serving bias-: Tendency of people to take credit for positive things but blame other or outside factors for negative events. This is a very common thing if you look at people around you. Example-: when a student scores good grade in class then he will credit this to his hard work and dedication but if he gets bad marks then he might blame that the teacher don't like him.

18) Spotlight effect-: Due to this bias people tends to think that there is a spotlight on them all the time which highlights all the mistakes and flaw in them. This happens because of being overly self-conscious, these people don't believe that people are different and have different perspectives. To overcome it, you need to first understand that – nobody is focusing on your flaws, you are the only one who always think about it which cause anxiety and stress, look around you will find that people are much busy in their own life no one is focusing on your flaws.

There are more than 190 cognitive biases and discussing all of them need me to write another book, but as we are living in the Internet era, you can easily explore more about it. Now we are going to discuss the logical fallacies which influence and distort our reasoning and logic.

Logical fallacies are errors in our reasoning and logic which make the debate or argument less effective. These fallacies mislead the argument, sometime these fallacies are used to intentionally manipulate or persuade the person with whom they were arguing, while sometimes people unintentionally use them because of a lack of knowledge about it. These fallacies are very common in mainstream media, politics and sales.

Now we are going to discuss types of logical fallacies -:

1. Straw man -: Misrepresentation of another person's argument by taking it out of context and exaggerating the arguments in an extreme way or by oversimplifying it. Concocting a false scenario and then attacking that scenario to make the opponent look bad.

Example-: Person (A)-: I think that human vehicles are contributing to global warming

Person(B) -: So, you think humans are directly causing extreme weather, causing drought in some places and cyclones in others. So you think that we should stop using our vehicles.

2. Slippery slope -: If we allow event A to happen then event Z will also consequently happens too, therefore event A should not happen. Fear-mongering is usually conveyed by these types of arguments. In this fallacy, a person who claims that one event will lead to another bad event should not let this happen.

Example -: If you don't give a vote to this candidate then your infrastructure, education, the health sector will never go to improve, so you should vote for this candidate.

3. Ad hominem -: When a person does not have anything logical to argue, then they start doing personal attacks on the characters of their opponent or we can say doing personal attacks on the characters or personal traits of your opponent to undermine their arguments.

Example- "You didn't have even finish school. How could you possibly know about this?" Here the educational level of the opponent is used as a means to exploit and degrade the argument.

4. Loaded question -: In this type of argument person asks a question that has already an assumption build into it so that it can be answered without appearing guilty. Assumption and conclusion are already built in it.

Example-: *Have you stopped drinking alcohol?

*Do you still beat your son?

5. False dichotomy (Black or white thinking) -: When only two options or alternatives are presented in an argument, when in fact more possibilities also exist. You are only left with an either-or position.

Example-: *Be my friend or be my enemy.

*If you are not with us, you are against us.

*If you are not a nationalist then you are anti-nationalist.

Here being neutral is not an option.

6. Circular argument -: In this argument when reasoning began with what they are trying to end with, there is no proof present, they just circulate the argument and it can easily be spotted because both sides of the argument are making the same point.

Using A to prove B then using B to prove A.

Example-: *The news is fake because so much news is fake.

*Everyone loves Aman because he is so much popular.

7. Red herring-: In this type of argument person try to misleads/ distracts by using emotions or using other ways from a relevant or important question asked by his opponent. Here person tries to manipulate or persuade you with emotions.

Example -: Suppose a mother and her daughter(age 6) had gone shopping, her daughter wants to buy a toy, then his mother tells her that let's rush home yummy treat is there for you. Her mother tries to distract her daughter attention from the toy.

8. Appeal to authority-: In this type of argument person uses the opinion of an authority on a topic as evidence to support his/ her argument. People usually think that if the authority had said this, it means that it must be true.

Example-: Celebrity opinion on a product.

Suppose a commercial brand claims that a specific brand of oats is the best way to start a day because cricketer Virat Kohli says that he eats every day in breakfast.

9. sunk cost fallacy -: The idea that a company/organization or people is more likely to continue with project/investment or real-life connection if they have already invested a lot of time, energy, money, effort in it even when continuing is not the best thing to do.

Example-:* watching a boring movie till the end

*When people stay in an unhealthy relationship even knowing that things are not going well.

It comes under logical fallacy because a person is logically aware that his decision is not worth it even he/ she invest in it.

10. Planning fallacy-: Tendency of person to underestimate the amount of time it will take to complete as well as cost and risk associated with it, even if it contradicts our his experience. Because of this fallacy in thinking people usually procrastinate so much and only work in a pressure state.

Example-: Let's say Ankit, a college student, has an examination on Saturday, a week from today. Ankit had already prepared for this type of time before and it usually takes him a week for preparation. However, he planned to slip the time and take 4 days rest and then start his preparation. He is positive that he will be able to complete his preparation in the last 3 days, so he starts it on Wednesday as planned earlier. In the end, he is not able to finish his preparation and isn't able to perform well in exams.

" Education must enable one to sift and weigh evidence to discern the true from false, the real from unreal and the facts from the fictions. The function of education, therefore, is to teach one to think intensively and to think critically."-:- Martin Luther King

XXIII
Mindset

Deep down we all know the importance of having the right mindset to achieve something in this real world. Our mindset determines how we are going to respond to certain situations like failure, rejections etc and also how we are going to overcome them. In the previous chapter, we had already discussed how high performing people approach things differently with their unique mindset compared to average performers. Just by changing your mindset, you can change the whole direction of your life. According to Stanford psychologist Carol Dweck (author of the book- mindset: The new psychology of success), our beliefs play a crucial role in our success and failure. Mindset is a belief that we formulated about our intelligence, talent, skills, personality and also about failure, challenges, competition surrounding us which influence how we feel, think and behave in certain situations.

According to Dweck, peoples mindset can be divided into two parts:

1) Fixed mindset (where you believe your abilities are fixed traits)

2) Growth mindset (where you believe your abilities can grow)

- **Fixed mindset**-: People with a fixed mindset believe that their qualities like intelligence, talent, skills, personality are fixed, inborn and unchangeable. So there is no way to improve them. A fixed mindset people wants to look smart and therefore to avoid any challenges, they easily give up when they face obstacles and also see efforts as a waste of time and energy. They avoid criticism, ignore useful negative feedback and feel threatened by the success of others. As a result of a fixed mindset, people achieve less than their full potential and usually end up being mediocre in life.

- **Growth mindset**-: People with a growth mindset believes that their qualities like intelligence, talent, skills, personality and character can be developed with hard work, effort and training.

A growth mindset leads to a desire to learn and therefore they tend to embrace challenges and see them as an opportunity to learn and develop, they persist in the face of setbacks and see failure as a chance to learn from their mistakes for the next attempt, learn from useful negative feedbacks and find lessons and inspiration in the success of others. As a result, they achieve higher in their field. These people usually have hunger for learning something new rather than a hunger for attention and approval.

Dweck found that the formation of mindset occurs in us mainly by two sources:- praising and labelling which both happen in our childhood.

From the experiment, Dweck found that kids behave differently depending upon the type of praising they receive after competing for the task(homework). Those children who get praising and labelling from parents or teachers that they are "smart" as they complete the task promotes a fixed mindset in them whereas those children who were praised for putting efforts promote a growth mindset in them. We are all aware that in our country usually parents and teachers praise us for the marks, as a result, many children have a default mode of fixed mindset from childhood. We can't blame our parents/ teachers for this because most of them are not even aware of this new concept of a growth mindset. Children should be taught to explore, be curious, embrace new experiences and challenges and try to learn from their mistakes.

We humans have two modes of thinking, first one is default mode (autopilot mode) which is operated by our subconscious. It includes our habits and going through the day without thinking much and the second mode is direct thinking which is operated by your consciousness – in this mode you control what you are thinking.

Every day you have a choice either to be in default mode and repeat what you are doing for a long time or either choose to think consciously which will evolve you. Being a conscious thinker is a skill that you can master with practice. Assuming that you are a right-handed person and now you have made a conscious choice that you want to be a left-handed person then in this case, firstly you will feel uncomfortable at the starting of a few months because for a long time you have trained yourself to be a right-handed person from your childhood. In the same way, when you try to come out of your default mode of thinking to a conscious thinker, you will need to deal with your limiting beliefs.

Limiting beliefs are thoughts and opinions that you consider absolute truth which is negatively affecting your life and also stop you from reaching your full potential. These beliefs usually come from your parents, teachers, your friends and the people around you who tell you that you are not good enough, you can't be liked or loved, you aren't able to do that work etc and sometimes these limiting beliefs are formed by your self by making a wrong conclusion from your breakup, failure, rejection etc. You need to first analyse the beliefs that you have and then you need to ask a question, did it serve me or negatively impact my life and stop me from reaching my full potential. From this method you will be able to find what are your limiting beliefs.

Examples of limiting beliefs -:

• I don't have a mathematical brain -: Just because you aren't able to love mathematics problems does not mean that you don't have a mathematical brain. The reality is that maybe you have never got a teacher in your life who had taught you things from basic or maybe you have got but you have never been dedicated to studying maths.

• I am not born for public speaking-: Who had told you that you are not born for it. Just because you aren't able to perform well in 2-3 public speaking does not mean that you are not born for it. You have yourself made a wrong conclusion about yourself and because of repetitively thinking, it becomes your belief. The reality is that you can learn and can do anything in your life. You just need the right path, hard work, patience, dedication and focus to achieve it.

• I don't deserve to be loved-: Just because you had gone through 2-3 breakups or rejections, you had concluded that you are not good enough to be loved, that is a wrong mindset. Maybe you are asking the wrong person to love you. The reality is that the world is big and there are so many people present on this planet, who want a partner like you.

These are the few examples but there are so many different types of limiting beliefs people hold which need to be recognized and changed.

XXIV
Upgrading with time

The main reason most people are not able to become better with time is that they are not upgrading and updating their knowledge, skills and personality with time. As people are not upgrading and updating, as a result, they are also losing many opportunities, which might have made them much more fortunate and wealthy.

For example- you have seen people around you, who are investing their money in older ways which might have been suitable for 50 years ago, as a result, these people are not getting better results and return from their investment. This happens because these people have not been updated and upgraded their knowledge of investment with time. You have also seen people who are so much shy and feel uncomfortable socializing etc, as a result, they miss so many great opportunities for their career and personal relationship which might have made their life much better. Maybe because of shyness he is not able to get into meaningful relationships. This happens because these types of people do not work on upgrading their personalities. It's okay that people are shy but if this trait starts adversely affecting their life then they need to work on it by socializing with more and more people. There are two ways by which you can explore your life and both of them are equally important. The first way is by going out and experimenting, learning from trial and error and personal experiences and the second one is learning from another person (by their books, podcasts, talking with them about their journey etc). The reality is that our life is short and if we don't learn from another person then we will end up wasting a lot of time. Maybe the things that you have learned by yourself by experimenting(trial and error) in 12 years is that same thing you might have been learned in just 5 years if you have learned from someone who had already travelled that path. Don't be a rigid person who doesn't upgrade with time, else your existence will fade away with time. Learning from the path of someone who had already achieved the thing that you wanted to achieve is a good thing.

Now we are going to talk about how you can upgrade your knowledge
- Reading books
- Listening to podcasts, from video clips
- Digital books and audiobooks
- Talking

Reading books -: How many books do you read every month aside from your academic books. If you are not reading any other books then you are losing a great chance to develop your mind. Everyone wants to be successful in life but if you don't grow your knowledge in your field, gather new perspectives to see the problem and have a mindset that is required, then how can you expect that one day you will be at the top position. In this era of the digital world, you will find that most people have lost the desire to read a book. Even though they download book in pdf format , most of them barely read them and very few people complete their books. The majority of us like to spend our time on social media, watching entertainment content on our devices rather than spending time reading a book. Watching an educational video on YouTube or reading a summary of books is good but there is so much difference between reading a book and watching a summary video. The authors of the book had done a lot of research to write a book and bind them into 200-500 pages, so YouTube video/summary article can give you the idea of books but don't think that a summary video can replace the real book. Another thing is that reading a book forces your brain to think deeply and imagine which mentally evolve you whereas most of book summary video doesn't provide deep thinking.

If you see wealthy people on this planet you will find one thing common in all of them that is the habit of reading a book. Almost 88% of wealthy people read 30 minutes or more every day. Rich and successful people are avid readers and have their specific reading routine. Warren Buffet spends 80% of their working day on reading, Bill Gates reads about 50 books in a year, Mark Zuckerberg reads about 2 books every month, Elon musk has a nightly ritual of reading a book before going to sleep. Reading books is a great way to expand your thinking, perspective and imagination.

From today make a resolution that you are going to create a reading habit and going to read different types of books. It's better to buy a physical book and read them. You can read different types of book in a different topic that fascinates you – it could be nonfiction, fiction books, biography and autobiography, books on mediation, health, yoga, spirituality, psychology, philosophy, history, finances, relationships, self-help books, coding, sci-fi, technology etc. Read books that you want to read, don't read books to look cool in someone else eye. Benefits of reading a book-:

• **Increase longevity by 23%** -: A study conducted on three groups of people, first those who read more than 3.5 hours per week, second were those who read books only for 3.5 hours per week and third were those who don't read any books.

It was found that those who read books more than 3.5 hours per week were 23% less likely to die compared to those who don't read at all. And those who read 3.5 hours per week were 17% less likely to die compared to those who don't study at all. So why do book readers live longer?

This happens because book reader undergoes " deep reading and thinking." Deep reading reduces cognitive decline and promotes emotional intelligence, social perception and empathy which leads to good social networks and better relationships. A good social network is associated with a higher survival rate as friends and family provide a source of comfort and support and also help us shield from stress and bring purpose into people's life.

• **Promote sleep and relaxation** -: Reading a book before going to sleep at night as a daily ritual help people to have a better sleep. It help our mind and body to relax. But make sure that you are reading a physical book because if you are reading from your device, it reduces the quality of sleep as our devices emit blue light which will disturb the circadian rhythm of our body.

• **Reduces our stress-:** Just reading a book for 30 minutes reduce your stress level by 68% compared to other activities like listening to music which reduces stress by 61%, drinking tea/ coffee (54%) and 30 minutes of walking only reduce stress by 42%. It slows down your heart rate, eases muscle tension and relaxes you.

- **Helps with depression:-** Research has found improvement in the mental health conditions of people who were going through depression when they read books. Especially self-help books.
- **Reduce the chance of Alzheimer and Parkinson disease -:** Readers are 2.5 times less likely to develop Alzheimer and other diseases related to memory and cognitive decline. In elderly people, it decreases mental decline by 32%.
- Boosts happiness

Above we discuss the benefits of reading books so that you can understand their importance.

When it comes to podcasts and audiobooks, these are a blessing that technology has provided us. First time in human history spoken words have reached as large scaled as books which had never happened before.

Both reading physical books and listening to podcasts has its advantage and disadvantages. Many people listen to podcasts while they are driving, travelling, running and doing exercises which is a better utilization of time. Podcasts are providing as much valuable content as a book and make a person think deeply about certain problems or topics. A great source to expand thinking capability and add new perspectives to see something. Sometimes we learn so many things from someone's journey of their success or failure, so try to spend time with someone with whom you can have a meaningful conversation.

Now you have started reading books, listening to podcasts, audiobooks, watching knowledgeable and good video content, and also spending time with people from whom you can learn so many things. There is another problem that arises is that you aren't able to retain information, to deal with this you need to have a journal where you make notes of the things that you learn and try to revise them from time to time.

XXV

Phone and social media are killing us

Now a day it seems like everyone is on social media and probably using a smartphone. On an average we spend 3-5hrs per day on the phone, if you don't believe it, then turn on the screen time app on your phone and see the result. By a survey, it is found that an average American checks their phone 96 times per day. In a survey by smartphone brand, it was revealed that the average Indian spend one-third of their waking hours on the phone, which translates to 1800 hours per year. As a result, most people complain that they do not have time for meditation, running, sleep, time for a relationship, hobbies etc as most of their time is wasted on their phone, many of us are not even aware of it. The reality is that most of us become addicted to social media and our phones, we can't imagine our life without them. Many people start their day by checking their phones and end their day with phones at night, these small habits affect our mood, self-respect, motivation in a bad way.

It costs time and money and makes your life worse. We need to accept the fact that our new generation is more immersed in this addiction loop. We have to reach a certain age to get legal access to alcohol but in the case of smartphones there are no such rules, we can't restrict it but we can teach children how to handle it carefully in a balanced way. Most parents give their children this weapon(phone) without teaching them how to handle it, as a result, they get into a self-destructive path. There is no doubt our phones are a great weapon as it has many benefits, but we should not ignore it's dark side also. Yes, parents should teach and make their children aware of cyberbullying, porn, sexting etc. You can use parental apps for your small child.

People who spend more time on social media application suffers a higher chance of getting depression than people who spend less time on it. The human brain functions in a certain irrespective of how intelligent and smart you are, many of these social media companies hire attention engineers who borrow principles from Las Vegas casino gambling and other places to try to make these products as addictive as possible so that they can maximize their profits.

These companies want you to use their apps in an addictive fashion so you spend more time and data on them.

We are all vulnerable to social proof, we care what other people think of us. When you upload a new photo of yourself on these apps then from that moment our minds get into a venerable state in knowing what other people think of your new photo. Social media releases a high amount of dopamine in our brain which makes it addictive. When you get a social media notification then your brain release dopaminergic which makes you happier at that moment. It creates a pseudo world of perfection where we can show our better or ideal version of our self, most of the photos/ videos have gone through so many filters and editing, peoples want to show how interesting, fun, happy, attractive they are. Though if you look at everyone on Facebook and Instagram then you might think all these peoples are so much happier, beautiful and then think I am not good looking and happier which will make you sad, lower your self-esteem and make you feel stressful etc. But in reality some of these happiest seeming people on social media are the saddest person in reality. Social media is not real, it doesn't show real 99% of our life behind the scene, normal unfiltered life, the reality is that no one looks perfect and happy all the time no matter how you are, sometimes you might feel stress, emotionally/ physically drained etc.

How social media and phone addiction is ruining your life

- Waste our time -: Most of us without even realising spends our day scrolling down these apps and constantly browsing, as a result you end up wasting lots of time which can be utilised in a more productive ways like exercise, hobbies, real relationship. Just open screen time on your phone, you will be shocked to see the time you spend every day.

- It kills motivation-: If you spend most time especially after waking up then you constantly supplying your brain with a high dose of dopamine as a result when you come back to do your work, you are not able to feel the same high and feel uninterested and laziness. You will compare your life either consciously or unconsciously with whom you followed and compare your normal life with the fake filtered world of others. You will compare your body, lifestyle with others which give birth to insecurities, sadness, makes you less satisfied with your life. You are comparing your life with something which is not real. You need to understand it and stop comparing, even if you want to compare your life you need to first set a good standard for it, compare your present with your past, see how much you had evolved based on skill, knowledge, experience, your appearance etc. If you just scroll down and spends most of your time on the phone then our brain register the fact that you have not taken any action towards your goals and at the end of the day it only gives you feeling of frustration, stress, lack of motivation.

• Dependent on positive reinforcement -: The views, likes and comments are all different kinds of positive reinforcement. Positive reinforcement means when someone rewards you for doing something good, example -: Imagine a child getting chocolate from parents after getting good marks on the test. Here parents reinforced their child to study more with positive rewards(chocolate).

In the same way in the virtual world, each comment and likes make you feel good about yourself, it tells your brain that someone in the world likes you, admires and appreciates you which boost self-worth, but the problem starts when you rely on social media to make you feel good, you stop appreciating your self and give control of your worth to others.

• Edit our life -: In our life, we all go with some important moment. Think of holidays, marriages etc we all don't want to forget this special moment of our life, so many of us take photos/ video to capture these moments. But when we post these photos on social media accounts, we stop focusing on the moment and start to edit these photos to appear perfect and strong to other people's. You edit photos, as a result, you create whole new stories and lost the actual special moment.

• Decrease concentration, focus and attention span when we spend time on the phone especially on social media apps then we are constantly excessing new data by just scrolling down in a very short time interval, as a result, your brain gets rewired to do multitask. It weakens your brain's ability to concentrate and focus on one thing and overall reduces your attention span.

How to balance social media and phones in our life?

1. **Take 30 days media detox challenge** -: Delete social media apps(Facebook, Instagram, Twitter, snapchat etc) from your phone. This challenge is not going to be easy but in the end, it is worth it. You might feel craving in 1st 10-15 days and feel like going back to the previous routine but after two weeks, things start getting normal, so you need a strategy to deal with cravings. Humans have a deep desire to be social and without it, there might be the chance you will get into depression, so you need to go out and spend your time with real people(friends and family), join the group so that you will be able to meet new like-minded people and able to create real connection, to hit the gym, go for running, surfing. When you are always on the phone most of the time, you will waste a good amount of time which you can spend on your hobbies, gaining new knowledge and skills which serve your growth and happiness. After 30 days when you complete your challenge then make a rule for phone or other devices use- turn off all notifications, and

have a fixed time block of day where you will use these apps, unfollow unnecessarily page and follow pages that provide you with knowledge and motivation.

Disconnect with those who drain your energy and put negativity in your mind.

2) Gradually reduce time on phone/social media -: Most people aren't able to quit social media suddenly. So it would be better to slowly move towards your goal. When you take 30 days social media detox challenge then in the first week, so just gradually reduce the time you spend on them. Let's say you are spending 4 hours on social media apps/ phone on an average then on 1st day just take a small step and reduce half an hour only, on 3rd day reduce another half an hour. You need to do it constantly and until you reach to 1-2 hours per day. Have a day in a week where you completely detach from social media so that you can self reflect about your life, make necessary decisions in distraction free environment.

XXVI
Daily nap

Yes, we all mostly love to sleep and do not want to leave that state. Good quality of sleep is the necessity of our body to heal itself to maintain a healthy mind and body. Some people see sleep as a waste of time and try to reduce the amount of sleep which mostly end up being sleep deprived, these people do not know that our mind and body get into a healing state, our brain and body detoxify harmful chemicals from our body, memory consolidation, muscle formation, hormone secretion happen while we sleep.

Chanakya had divided 24 hours into 16 parts each for 90 minutes. He had created a strict routine for Chandragupta Maurya which is required to build a great empire, he suggests that between 9-10 PM one should go to bed for sleep and wake up at 1:30 AM and starts his day with meditation. He suggested sleeping four and a half hours during the night and in the afternoon between 1:30 PM to 3 PM one should take a nap.

So the total rest time including sleep and nap equals 6 hours, which is good sleep for an average person. He does believe in the quality of sleep over quantity. He believes in early to bed and early to rise for maintaining good health. He also suggested having a ritual of listening to music before sleep as it soothes the mind and gives calmness. Chanakya believes in a biphasic sleep pattern. Biphasic sleep refers to a sleep habit that involves a person sleeping for two segments.

Sleeping during the night and taking a midday nap. Today society puts so much focus on taking a straight 6-8 hours of sleep, there is nothing wrong with it. But many of us feel the downfall of energy, motivation and willpower in the afternoon. So why not divide your day into two productive parts by practising biphasic sleep patterns. We have a biological clock (circadian rhythm) that program our body when to sleep, so maintaining consistency is needed while practising biphasic sleep. You need to first fix your time for sleep at night and also have a fixed time for nap else if you constantly make changes in your sleep time then your biological clock gets confused as a result you might feel low energy, low motivation, unable to focus and concentrate, less willpower, drive the whole day and also our biological clock regulates our mood, so if you are sleep deprived you will have mood swings. This will adversely affect your physical and mental health. So maintaining a fixed sleep schedule is important irrespective of sleep pattern(monophasic or biphasic). We need to understand that we all do different types of physical works which require different efforts, so the amount of sleep varies from person to person. Let's say you go to a gym every day, so to recover your muscles you need more sleep compared to a person who doesn't go to a gym.

You need 7-8 hr sleep to properly recover your muscle. The amount of sleep mostly depends upon your daily physical activity, quality of food and how you manage stress and deal with trauma. There might be a chance that you had altered your biological clock and may not feel low every between(1 PM- 3 PM) but there will be a time where you feel low every take nap in that time.

There are different types of naps according to their length, choose according to your need -:

- 20- 25 minutes nap(power nap) -: This is an optimal time for a nap, ideal for boosting alertness, motor learning skills like playing the guitar Do not go for 30 minutes nap it will lead to a feeling of grogginess and hangover.

- 40-60 minutes nap -:This nap will help you to improve memory power and enhance your learning ability. But the problem with this nap is that you will feel grogginess after you wake and this feeling may continue till 1-2 hours. But if want to take this nap and want to over grogginess then take coffee after you wake up, expose yourself to the sun or go again to take a 90-minute nap.

- 90-minute nap-: This nap will boost your creativity, improve memory and emotions. This 90-minute cycle of sleep includes a lighter and deeper level of sleep. This nap may include REM (Rapid eye movements) which is a link to the dreaming stage. After you wake up you will feel no grogginess and with fresh and calm mood.

The best advice is to take either 20 minutes nap or go for 90 minutes so that when you wake up to there is no grogginess and you will feel fresh.

But a nap is not for everyone especially not for those who are suffering from insomnia or have trouble while sleeping in the night.

How to take a successful nap

1) Create an environment -: Most people say that they are not able to take small sleep(nap) during the afternoon, the major reason is that they do not care about the environment. Creating an environment for nap-: It's really important to ensure a place where there is no noise or less noise. Make the room darker with the help of a window curtain or you can use eye masks. It's important to dark the room because exposure to the sunlight inhibits melatonin production, a vital hormone that regulates our sleep.

2) Set the alarm -: If you don't set the alarm then there will be a most possible chance that you will oversleep and ends up feeling groggy after you wake up. Set peaceful music as an alarm tone.

XXVII

Luck

Yes, we all want to be lucky.

Is there any way by which you can enhance your luck?

There are mainly three types of luck -:

1) Luck which is created by circumstances or environment -: Let's understand with an example-: suppose you have gone to your friend's marriage ceremony, you meet a girl there and after over period you start dating her then after some time she becomes your girlfriend and after some time you both get married.

Here environment/ circumstance-: " was friend's marriage but you luckily meet a girl".

That girl is an opportunity for you and you reacted to that opportunity by asking her out and dating her and that results in your marriage.

In the same way in life, we all get so many big or small opportunity and the person who act or grab these opportunities become lucky and create a good future. But the problem with most people is that they are not aware and prepared for upcoming opportunities . As a result they lose the chance to create good luck for themselves.

2) Luck which is created by birth-: Yes, we all have taken birth to different- different types of family background (born into poor, middle class, rich), raised into different types of environment, and also faced different-different challenges.

But suppose you had born in a rich and educated family then there is a probable chance that you will face very fewer problems compared to those who were born in a poor and uneducated family etc. In this type of luck, we have no control, so you can't do anything about it but you can create a good or dream future with your ability and hard work.

3) Luck by chance / passive luck-: Passive luck includes winning a lottery, getting money while walking on the road. In this type of luck, we have no control.

From above all three types of luck, we only have control over some extent to the luck which is created by environment/circumstance.

So, the question arises is there any way by which we can enhance our luck, and the answer is yes. There are some ways mentioned below by which we can enhance our luck.

1. Whenever you get the opportunity then you should grab that and should act upon it by putting your efforts, dedication, hard work and planning etc. You should appreciate it that only you can create good luck for yourself. But most of the time people are not aware and not prepared for the opportunity. As a result, they lose golden chances in their life. Remember

" Fortune favours the prepared mind" – Louis Pasteur
Simple formula -:
Whenever you see an opportunity -> Appreciate it -> Act on it

By this, you will be able to make and create luck which is given to you by environment/ circumstance/ situations. You need to maximize your opportunities by being open to new experiences, maintain contact with a broad network of people. Those people become usually lucky who constantly looks for new opportunities, they look for better and they believe that there is a possibility on every corner, you just need to find out.

" Luck is being in the right place, at the right time, by doing the right thing. How? By being in the right state of mind"

2) Your luck increases when you are in a high vibrational state-: Everything in this universe is made up of energy and everything is vibrating at a certain frequency level. A normal person body has a frequency of (60-72MHz). When the vibration of the body goes down from 60 MHz then you start feeling sadness, anger, depressed and you start to attract negativity from the universe. While when your body is in high vibrational state (that is faith, love, happiness, joy, calm, sexual energy) then you can attract positivity from the universe.

So we need to be in a high vibrational state to attract good things and be lucky.

There are some ways by which we can maintain a high vibration

• Music-: Not all types of music, but music that makes you feel good, feel positive, feeling of love and romance and encouraging music help us to feel good and helps to enhance the vibration. Calm and peaceful instrumental music has very good effects.

• Working on things, you are passionate about-: Maybe you like dancing, painting or playing any musical instruments or have any other hobbies. All these activities help you to enhance your vibrational state.

• Meditation, yoga and exercises -: These activities helps you to enhance your consciousness and gives you a happy and calm feeling which raises your vibration.• Stop negative thinking -: The more you surround yourself with negative peoples the less you feel happy and which result in low vibration. You can't think positive if you are always surrounded by negative people who give you doubt, lower your standard, disrespect you, talk negatively etc, so it's important to first eliminate negative people from your life.

• Gratitude -: More you are grateful for the things you have in your life, the happier you become. A grateful heart is a powerful magnet for positive things. Start showing gratitude every day to maintain happiness and a high vibrational state.

3) Turn your bad luck into good luck-: Bad luck can happen to anyone but lucky people usually focus on the positive side after getting failure or facing any adverse situation. They try to find positivity and lesson from their experiences so that they can bounce back with their new updated version. But the problem with most people is that after getting a failure or facing any bad situations they start to think negative and focuses just on the negativity.

4) Listen to your lucky hunches -: Yes, lucky people rely on their strong intuitions, when a person sets himself in a positive vibration and focus on his something with great desire then universe starts guiding him to move forward. These guiding usually comes to us mostly by intuition.

XXVIII
Let's talk about porn

The main aim of this chapter is to make you aware of the reality of porn.

Let's talk about pornography, we all know about it and almost 90% of people know about it. 30% of internet search are about porn, and 35% of total downloads is porn.

India is third the largest consumer of porn in the world, even though no one wants to talk about it and view it as a taboo topic. Teenager is the largest consumer of porn, and 1/3 of porn in India are consumed by women.

First, we need to understand why people go into porn again and again. Mostly because of three reasons -:

1. Boredom/ loneliness-: This mostly happens to a person when he/she is following a routine to accomplish their task and they get boredom just by repeating that every day. The brain analyses that you are not doing anything exciting, as a result your brain tries to find an easy way to get excitement and dopamine high, as a result, you get into it. Your brain uses it as escapism from your work and procrastinate.

Solution-: The solution is to release feel-good hormones from your body which can be done when you start doing exercise, running, working out. You can also involve in things which you are passionate about such as dancing, playing instruments, playing games etc. You need to do it every day.

2. To meet sexual fantasy-: Porn can full fill any type of unrealistic sexual fantasy which can never be fulfilled in the real world. As a result consumption of porn starts rewiring your brain in such a way that it responds to only a certain stimulus when a fantasy is meeting, which can't be possible in real sex. Also, there are large choices available based on different fantasy which trigger and stimulate our brain so much because our brain love choices.

Solution-: You need to understand that porn is selling you body insecurity and the actors/actress of porn go through so many surgeries and medications to look that much perfect. Due to this, you judge your own body and your partner's body

Many people disagree and say that they get sex education from porn, but the actual reality is they are getting an education on rape because 70% to 85% of porn shows violence and abuse.

" Watching porn to learn about sex is like watching a hospital drama show to learn how to be a doctor"

3. Another reason you are watching so much porn is because of trauma, there might be a chance that you had gone through an emotionally disturbing situation that had impacted you. So you are using porn as an escape/distraction from your trauma. You might use porn as a coping mechanism to escape from trauma.

Solution-: You need to find the deep cause which is causing the compulsive use of porn. Try to go deep with yourself by asking questions, so that you can find the cause of trauma. You can try journaling to heal from trauma else you need to meet a physiotherapist to solve your trauma.

If 90% of people watch porn then in this 90% about 1-2% of people will be going to use sexual violence by going outside and doing rape, marital rape is also included in it because people are not educated about porn.

As we all know, when a person compulsively and continuously starts watching porn then he does not watch the same clip every time because his brain does not release the same amount of dopamine that he got from the first clip, as a result, to get more dopamine he switches to more porn including more violence and darker content as a result person end up developing a dark fantasy.

These dark fantasies include-: forced Hardcore, violence, BDSM, anal fisting, incest etc. As a result demand for more hardcore, humiliated and violent porn increased, due to this human trafficking was done, drugs were given to a kidnapped person to shoot a violent porn video.

Porn stars do not agree to shoot violent porn, so the porn industry does human trafficking to make a video.

As a porn consumer who full fills his dark fantasy, you are indirectly demanding the porn industry to make these videos and indirectly supporting sexual violence, human trafficking, rape and child pornography.

You need to understand that porn has become a billion-dollar industry and going to do anything to make a profit.

You need to consciously decide whom you are going to choose and support. You need to accept the fact that our country comes under developing countries – even though the internet and porn are widespread, the majority of people even does not have any basic sex education which makes thing more dangerous. Porn had existed long before the digital revolution but it was not that easily accessible but after the digital revolution, things had changed – there is mass content available with just a few clicks. Our generation is the first generation that has so much easy accessibility of porn. So it's become really important that we manage it carefully without causing any adverse effects on us.

There are so many porn sites and each site generally contain a minimum of 25 categories and in each category, there are thousands of videos, as humans we like options, but in porn, these option traps you and makes you an addict. Yes, porn gives you an idea of sex but actually what kind of ideas it gives you, go through a top porn website then on their home page there is incest(sexual relations between family members or close ones), you will find forced sex which is rape.

About 94% of aggression targets are women and out of this 95% responded to this aggression as pleasurable and normal. Yes, porn does add ideas about sex but many of these ideas are unhealthy, unethical and illegal.

You all need to have standards for human relationships that you will never going to break but incest porn motivates you.

Research has found that gays are degraded because of female traits in most porn.

About 70% of people have seen non-consensual porn.

Yes, porn is a teacher but not a good one. Protection, consent, safety are not learned by mainstream porn.

We must talk about porn it's a non-negotiable topic.

Names of rape victims become trending in top porn websites, more than eight million times their names were searched on porn websites. This makes me ashamed of being part of this society, there are so many sick mentalities of people present around us, we are just unaware of it. Porn is something which is a major reason for the development of these levels of the darker world, our country is so much suppressed when it comes to sex, no one wants to talk about it but in their inner world, they are trapped into porn and had developed the darkest fantasy which any normal person could not imagine. Our brain is so much complex it's okay to have a normal fantasy but don't connect your porn fantasy with your real life.

The only reason people had developed fucked-up fantasies is that they had made a porn regular and frequent source of fun and got deep into it.

Many people have a fantasy of incest due to frequent consumption of incest porn, as a result, it becomes their dominating thought and due to this, their brain starts connecting incest fantasy with real-life which actually makes them feel uncomfortable and also degrades their relationship with family members.

The solution is simple, you need to first stop consuming that specific porn fantasy type that is triggering your mind and you need to divert your focus on something really important it could be your carrier goal (clearing exam), something you are passionate about like playing musical instruments, learning a martial art, involving in any type of art depending upon your own choice or you can make new friends etc.

So that the priorities of your life change. You need to accept the fact that human sexuality is so much complex, no one completely knows what can trigger it. Fantasy is okay if you learn to control and manage them.

There is always a need for sets of rules and boundaries, to manage your fantasies or your kink.

As biological beings, we try to extract pleasure from everything. So as you are living comfortably in your house and getting all the resources for survival, then your brain goes to the second step which is reproduction because your brain wants to pass your genes forward. We all need to understand and accept that desire for sex is normal. Yes, we are biology being and we all have a deep desire for sex, it's all okay and normal to get into masturbation and watch porn occasionally but it becomes a problem when it becomes the core of your life and you are compulsively involved in it. Let's say you are single and you watch porn once or twice a month to fulfil your sexual desire and fantasy then that's okay. But don't make porn a frequent source of fun and excitement else you will stuck in a loop of compulsively watching porn.

As a human, we learn things from watching but when we watch porn due to mirror neuron it make us feel while watching that we are experiencing the things which make our monkey brain think that we have an unlimited or large number of sexual partner and we can have as much sex as we want. This whole thinking is done by our monkey brain.

This chapter aims to make you come out of compulsive behaviour and make you aware of the actual reality of the porn industry.

To come out of this compulsive behaviour, you need to first admit it.

Follow this to come out of pornography -:

• Resist access -: Delete porn folder from your device, and start using porn blocking website and also remove the pages you have liked in Instagram(Instagram models are making you fool these models have gone through plastic surgeries . Photos were gone through so many filters and the photo is also taken in a way to look more sex appealing which rewires you and changes the whole perception of sexuality, as a result, you do not find women attractive in actual real-world). Remove everything from your device which triggers you.

- Make friends with the opposite gender and try to know their emotional sides, bond with them it will reshape your perspective and also you able to understand women. Because porn rewires the male brain to objectify the female body. Improve your social life make new friends or hang out with existing friends.
- As porn produces high dopamine, try to replace it with something which gives the same high dopamine level. Example – working out, running, dancing etc.
- Pursue your life goals and get busy accomplishing them – Porn is most dangerous as it destroys your dopamine receptor as a result you get less motivation to work towards your real-life goals.

" Everything is boring in the life of porn addict except porn "

- Decide it and finally quit it -: Make your willpower win, finally quit it-famous people Terry crews, Russell Brand etc have done it. In your mind tell yourself that you are not quitting, you are just going for a break and as time passes compulsion will be less and it will be easy for you to quit it.
- Power of sex transmutation – I encourage you to take the 90-day Nofap challenge, I promise you will see visual change. It helps your brain to heal from porn.
- Most people do not want to quit porn forever, for them my suggestion is to start seeing porn as a drug and reduce its consumption and set limits for it. Learn to regulate it. You should always ask yourself that is it harming you

someway. What type of pornographic content I am watching if I am working towards my purpose in life, how much is it affecting my life, what is its impact on me.

· Start masturbating with your imagination so that it does not affect your normal dopamine level of the brain to a great extent.

And does not affect your motivation for this real world.

To quit porn, you need to first make a change in the mindset about

How you view porn- you need to associate the feeling of pain in watching porn, see porn as something which is degrading your life and this is the first step in process of quitting porn because most peoples are comfortable about porn and see it as a sexy thing.

" You need to get better for yourself man"

You need to develop a game plan for how you are going to tackle the desire for porn, you need to find out what are the things which trigger this behaviour in you it might be someplace, some specific time etc. You need to analyse all the things which drive you into this behaviour.

After finding the cause of the behaviour you need to make changes in your routine. For example -: If you search porn before going to sleep (here sleep time is a trigger) then you need to stop using the phone and instead you can read a book.

Some time sexual abuse in early childhood, being raised in a toxic environment and getting less love is also causing the development of porn addiction, you need to go deeper within yourself to find the root cause.

How to quit porn is the wrong way to think about it. The right way is to try to figure out how to have a better life.

" I am not quitting porn, I am striving for a better life"- Jordan Peterson

You need to have a vision for your future life that is more compelling than porn.

You need to ask yourself how your life will positively change in the upcoming 5 years if you quit porn(how your relationships, career, your purpose will change) also you need to have a vision for your future life that how will your life looks like in the upcoming 5 years if you do not quit porn how your relationships, careers will going to suffer.

Porn is dangerous because it offers immediate gratification but no medium for long term character development and life.

Life is short, and you had already wasted so much time in porn and doing stupid things, now it is time to make a change in the quality of your life and it's time to make it more exciting and full of purpose.

Give your time to your hobbies (dancing, painting, sports) and in improving your knowledge and skills, it's time to cultivate your brain and become a more intellectual person, travel etc. When you start focusing on your improving your intellectual life, ideology life, academic life, relationships life, social life and many other then you will be easily detached from porn.

You are doing nothing in life or maybe doing the job just for money and living your life with no purpose and at the end of the day to gain excitement(dopamine high) you get into porn and masturbation to get easy fun. Lethargic life will drive you toward porn addiction. You need to grow as a person in your life and make it more exciting, fun and full of happiness and satisfaction which only happen when you are working to build the life that you want to live, rather than going for instant gratification.

The reason why you should quit porn

- It destroys productivity and focus- We all know that focus takes time to build, if you are into porn then you can't work, you will take so much time to do small things and also develop procrastination.

Average male porn addict watches 4- 12 hour porn per week that's an entire working day wasted on it that you will never get back.

- It causes erectile dysfunction, premature ejaculation and delayed ejaculation – why most men do not understand that porn cause changes in your brain, which happen at a subconscious level and the problem is porn is fake and create unrealistic belief and perception far from reality.
- Causes social anxiety and low self-esteem
- Promote violence against women

The ultimate aim of this chapter was to make you aware of porn, help you to come out of any type of compulsive behaviour. Even if you want to indulge in it then it's your personal choice but always practice moderation. The future of the porn industry can be ethical porn which is going to be far much better than mainstream porn. If you want to watch porn go for ethical porn.

XXIX

Sexting, sextortion and revenge porn

No one talks about it and many are unaware of these matters. As technologically we have evolved, so many changes have occurred, one of the huge changes happened to the relationship dynamic, now the gap between peoples have reduced so much, as a result sexting has become popular especially among teenagers. As intimate relationship expands through the technological platform, teenagers are finding a new way to explore their sexuality.

Sexting is sending or receiving sexually explicit(nudes) photos, videos or messages between two or more groups of people with the help of phones, computers, webcams or other devices. Studies have shown that one out of five teens has sent sexually explicit photos or videos. 51% of those who have sent a sext are teen girls who felt pressure from a guy compared to the 18% of teen boys who felt pressure from girls.

Minors who send sexually explicit photos are at risk of child pornography. There is a strict rule for child pornography in every country. Child pornography law was created to protect children from exploitation and abuse.

Reason for sexting-: There are so many reasons people engage in sexting or are encouraged or pressured to do so. According to reports-:

• Half of teen girls cited pressure from teen boys to do sexting.

• Peer pressure is also one of the causes, 23% of girls and 24% of boys said that they were pressured by friends to send their explicit photos.

• Some send them as a joke or dare, teens might send a photo of themselves as a way of flirting with potential partners to get compliments.

• Some teens think that it's cool to have a nude photo of their girlfriend/boyfriends.

*Many girls said that they do sexting to sustain the relationship as many girls have a fear that if they don't do it then they will lose the relationship.

Many do it to prove their commitment and devotion to their partners.

• It can be done for purposes of bullying or humiliating another person. This might be done after a relationship end.

Disadvantages of sexting

Sexting gives origin to two crimes: sextortion and Revenge porn.

1. Sextortion-: It's a serious crime that occurs when someone threatens to distribute or leak your private and sensitive material if you do not provide them with your images or videos of sexual nature, sexual favour or money.

Report from research tells us –

• That 60% of perpetrators are familiar with the victim(friends, ex-boyfriend, classmates etc.) and 40% of victims meet perpetrators online(from social media).

- Most adult victims of sextortion are females. Both the genders of society are vulnerable to the crimes of sextortion.

2. Revenge porn-: It refers to the sharing or spreading of sexually explicit images or videos without the consent of the person in the image. It is a huge crime. Revenge porn increases because of the increase in sexting.

Prevention -: Don't allow your partner to take any sexually explicit images or videos.

Cause-

When the relationship ends with a breakup or divorce, some criminal-minded individuals choose to use sexually explicit images/ videos that they have of their ex-partner as a means to take revenge on them by spreading their intimate photos. In general, it means uploading sexually explicit images to humiliate and degrade the person, who has broken off the relationship.

This result in loss of reputation which sometimes leads to the loss of their job and gets his/ her character Judge by society.

This all leads the victim to gets into mental trauma, depression, humiliation , social isolation, low self-worth, negatively impact on the psychology of victim, loss of trust issues, suicidal thoughts.

Yes, people in our society are so much judgemental but this mindset of peoples need to improve. In our country, people will focus less on the criminal but doubt and judge more on the victim (women).

How to protect from sextortion and revenge porn

- Stop talking or having some contact with strangers -: In a lot of cases, people come in contact with an unknown person through social media, dating and matrimonial apps. The profile they contacted is mostly fake. The person behind the profile is a criminal whose main motive is to extort money, sexual favour from the victim. There might be proper racket going on. These fake profiles are purposefully made to look very attractive so that people fall prey to scam easily.

The person who operates these accounts talks to the victim normally for few days to establish a friendship or relationship and then after that, they encourage the victim to share their intimate, nude photos or videos, sexual in video calls with them.

Once the criminal has access to private materials then they start blackmailing the victim and asks for money or sexual favour. This crime can be committed by someone with whom the victim had an intimate relationship in the past. Sometimes such people get access to private photos/videos of the victim and when the relationship ends they use it to extort money or sexual favour from the victim.

Safety precautions

• Never talk or connect with strangers, even though the person in profile looking so beautiful or handsome.

Now a days peoples are so much obsessed to have followers in their social media accounts, don't give access to unknown person especially without having real photos on their profile.

• Never allow anyone, however close that person may be to capture your private photo or intimate activity with any device. Such data can be misused at a later stage to blackmail you. No one knows your today's lover/boyfriend can be the future blackmailer. But as they say, love is blind, criminals can be extremely manipulative.

• Always remember the internet never forget and forgive. If you had shared something once on the Internet then it will always be present in some form. The reach and speed of the internet are tremendous, the objectionable material can spread to millions in a very short span.

• If you give your phone or device to someone always keep care of your data, delete it or encrypt it so that when someone tries to access the encrypted personal data then they would not be able to recover it without a password or pin.

Do not let it be open, it can be misused in some way. Criminal can Photoshop them to harm your reputation. Always use strong passwords in your accounts and devices. Cover your webcam when it is not in use because one of the most strange cases of sextortion is done by hacking the webcam.

How to deal with sextortion

• Don't panic-: Most of the time victims gets into so much panic, become stressed and overthink so much of being judged, have fear how people will react. Every things will be okay as time goes. You do not need to be trapped in negative thinking, you have not done anything wrong, it's the perpetrator who needs to be punished.

• Tell someone close to you-:Reach out for help from your trusted family members and friends. So that they guide you to take a good decision and helps you to file complaints in the police station. Remember you are the victim of a nasty abuser who is relying on your silence to continue the assault.

• Stop all contact with perpetrators -: Block them in all the social media accounts, you can deactivate your account for some time but do not delete as you may lose evidence.

• Collect the evidences-: Do not try to delete any type of email demanding money, or any message from the perpetrator, take screenshots, keep a record of all contact from the blackmailer as they are the proofs and evidences which helps police to catch the criminal.

- Immediately go to police -: Go to the police and tell them your story and present the evidence you had collected, as police are connected with cybersecurity they catch the criminal. One of the huge issues with sextortion cases is that most of them were not reported. Just because of fear of being judged, losing reputation, as a result victims get assaulted so many times. People need to change their mindset and the way they perceive sextortion.

- Never pay-: Do not give money or send any sexually explicit photos of yourself. Giving into demand will make things worse because paying in demand will result in more demand for money or your sexual photos.

Impact of sextortion

- Sextortion affect the psychology of victim so much, they feel ashamed of themselves, having a fear of being judged by society, get in depression, mental trauma and stressed, get into negative thinking which sometimes results in self-harming tendencies and suicide. So it's important to give a good environment to the victim so that he/ she will heal from it. Psychological treatment can be helpful.

XXX
Training sexuality

Humans have forgotten the blessings of the power of sexual energy which can raise them above the rest. Rather than positivity , people associate so much negativity with it. Most people especially men, are not trained and also not aware of this superpower inside them. Because from society, people only get knowledge of the physical expression of sexual energy. Transmuting this energy in other areas of life will act as a miracle.

Transmuting sexual energy means switching your mind from thoughts of physical expression to the thought of other nature. Example-: Transmuting this energy into creating a business, being a world-class actor, athlete, painter, singer etc.

Sex transmutation is beautifully explained by Napoleon Hill in his book " Think and grow rich".

When driven by this desire, men develop keenness of imagination, courage, willpower, persistence and creative ability unknown to them at other times. Sex energy is the creative energy of all geniuses. There never has been and never will be a great leader, artist lacking in the driving

force of sex.
-: Napoleon hill

This energy is the main source of motivation and ambition in humans.

By destroying the sex gland in the man, you will find his major source of motivation to take action have been removed. The desire for sexual expression is inborn and natural, the desire should not be eliminated or ignored.

The emotion of sex can be controlled for some time, but it tries to seek expression, so if it does not transmute it will seek out physical expression(sex, masturbation). Remember there is nothing wrong with expressing your sexual energy in physical form but it's limited. Also, there is nothing wrong with being limited. It's your life, so it's your own choice. But it becomes a problem when you overindulge in it, just like anything.

Scientific studies have revealed that men of greatest achievement are the men who learned sex transmutation, these are the men who accumulated great wealth, achieved greatness in literature, art etc.

The love story of Abraham Lincoln -: The relationship and its impact on Lincoln is depicted as one of the greatest love stories of all time. Lincoln and a lady named Ann had developed a romantic attraction for each other, but that woman was engaged with another man.

But the impact of Ann on his life was so much that it left him with lifelong melancholy and even raised him to political greatness.

"Her memories were enough to rise him to greatness"

Story of Napoleon Bonaparte-: History is filled with the records of great achievers whose creative faculty of mind are aroused by the influence of women. Napoleon was one of these. When he was inspired by his wife Josephine he was unbeatable. But when he put Josephine aside, he began to lose wars.

Remove all women from the earth and you will find that 80% of men will lose their motivation to act, accumulated wealth and achieve high because unconsciously and indirectly women in our life and surrounding greatly affect our motivation.

Human mind response to stimulation like –

1)Desire for sex

2) love

3) desire for fame, power, Money

4) Music

5) Alcohol and drugs

But the desire for sex is most powerful.

" It's very hard to beat a man who is focused and driven by his emotional energy(love, romance, anger, pain or any trauma) towards his purpose.

More than 80 years had passed away as "Think and grow rich " was first published in 1937 but still the majority of people till now are not able to understand completely about sex transmutation. Napoleon hill does not tell us to suppress our sexual urge inside yourself nor he said not to involve in any type of sexual activity but he wants to tell us that – sexual energy is not just limited to physical expression, when this energy is redirected then it had potential to brighten the other area of your life.

So the question arises – what is sex transmutation?

It simply means just focus on the specific goal that you want to achieve – it can be anything such as starting a business and growing it, creating music, selling any product, writing a book etc and forget about sex for a certain period. As you stop your physical expression of your sexual energy, that energy which is still present inside you will act as a motivation or driving force to accomplish your goal. Forgetting about sex means – you are not going to express your sexual energy in physical form (sex, masturbation) nor you are going to waste your time thinking about sex.

A massive and stupendous amount of thinking goes into sex without the act of procreation – Elon musk

As our lot of time goes thinking about sex, so it's really important that when you are practising Nofap or semen retention you are not compulsively thinking about sex and just retaining your sexual energy. It is important to let go of sexual thoughts. Even if you are restricting from sexual activity, you are thinking about sex then it's the wrong way of doing a Nofap, as you are wasting a lot of your mental energy on thinking about sex. I am not telling you that you will not be going to have sexual urges as if you look around especially in the digital industry – Facebook, Netflix, easy access to porn, Instagram.

The majority of things had been sexualized. You can't fight with your sexual urges nor you will be able to suppress them for a long time – your only work is to accept your sexual desire but not to act on them and let them go. The majority of people fail in nofap because they try to suppress their desire which ends up in frustration, lack of focus, low concentrations, trouble sleeping, anxiety and many other issues. Discusses nofap below -:

This energy gives a superpower for action. But if a man is driven alone by the desire of sex man may steal, cheat and even commit murder but when the emotion of love and romance is mixed then man will guide his action with balance and reasons.

"When a man is driven by the blend of these three stimuli – love, romance and sex(not in a physical

expression) then it has the potential to raise him to a great height, it will enrich him with persistence, focus, clarity, courage, calmness and creativity. That creativity will open the door of infinite intelligence for him."

Nofap can change your life and help you in achieving your goals. Many successful people are using this method to boost their focus and energy.

Either you are a focused person or you are a failure there is nothing in between -Vivek Bindra

Nofap is quite simple: no porn, no masturbation from porn but can have sex in moderation. Let engaging in sexual activity is your conscious choice. Tell yourself that you are going for a break from sex for a certain period. Nofap works because our majority motivation for doing daily tasks depends upon hormones which affect our physiological and behaviour to some extent. When we starve for sex for a certain period, then our brain and body get into a problem-solving mode in real life or action mode to get that ultimate pleasure, while solving problems, we end up doing so many things and achieving results. So everyone should practice nofap in their life it could be for 1, 2, 3 or 4 months.

Even if you don't want to do it

" Just try it for 30 days in a year"

Nofap helps to rewire the brain and helps to recover the brain from the damage caused by porn, as porn had rewired the brain to get the ultimate pleasure of life effortlessly with just a few clicks and seeks instant gratification. While nofap teaches us delayed gratification and patience which are the most important things to get success in real life.

As porn has destroyed the dopamine receptor which results in a lack of motivation, cause mood swings, stress, social anxiety, cause of depression, inability to focus, weak willpower and determination. Nofap heals all the things.

What is the need for Nofap? Do it because you want to enhance the quality of your life, want to be more focused which boosts work/skill productivity, want to heal yourself from compulsive use of porn, want to become a better version of yourself. Don't do it to boost your ego by telling another person that you are in nofap, for getting more girls, for getting more attention.

" In the world full of distraction, if you are focused you will win"

Remember nofap is great for a person who gets easily distracted from their goals, there is a misconception spreading in the society that doing – Nofap or semen retention makes you successful, but that is not the actual reality, to be successful in your work you need – Focus, dedication, smart thinking, hard work, clarity, faith, habits, persistence. But definitely, if nofap / semen retention is done in the right way it will amplify your speed to reach your goals. If you are thinking that Nofap alone will make you successful then it's the wrong way of thinking about it. As there is no direct connection between sex and success in life. Now a days, on the internet there is propaganda going on that nofap/ semen retention give you mystic power that is completely false for the majority of peoples. They just talk about few name like swami Vivekananda, Steve Jobs, Tesla etc and tell that these people practice semen retention which makes them successful, but thousands of other personality does not practice semen retention also become successful while having a normal sex life.

There is no doubt that practising celibacy give you an advantage in the spiritual journey and can also give you mystic powers but you need to understand that celibacy is not for everyone. Only 2-3% of the population reading this may choose this path.

The problem with humans is that we waste a lot of energy and time thinking about sex till our hormones are at their peak and after a certain age (after the thirties) things get normal. As a result, we accumulate major wealth in the later age of our life.

The ultimate goal is not to make sex the core of your life, it's just a part of life and we should not make it a big thing nor we should overthink about it, it's a part of life.

When sex gets into your mind it becomes a problem because you will waste a lot of time, energy, money on compulsive behaviour.

Sex in the body is fine. Money in the pocket is fine. They only become a problem if they enter your mind.- Sadhguru

You can become powerful and can grow spiritually when you do certain types of yogic practice (kundalini yoga) while practising semen retention to raise energy. Semen retention is not for everyone, but you should try it once or experiment with yourself for a certain period. If you feel that it helps you in becoming more spiritual, focus and dedicated towards your goal, you can continue.

It's very important to do semen retention in the right way because it is something that can give your tremendous benefits or may harm you if done in the wrong way. It is important to circulate/ raise your sexual energy in the body, so it's not just about holding your semen but other practices like mediation and sadhana, yoga's (kaya Kalpa yoga, kundalini yoga), specific exercises to maintain prostate health, becoming vegetarian, realising trauma which had created energy blockages, self-reflection etc, needs to be done if you choose to do semen retention/celibacy for a long time. Then only you will able to get the advantage of it else you are on the wrong path.

But you should try Nofap, it's for everyone.

There is no doubt that great personalities like Swami Vivekananda, Nikola tesla practice celibacy (semen retention) but they also involve in meditation and yogic practices. No doubt practising celibacy can lift someone to greater heights in spirituality, can give mystic powers, give access to infinite intelligence, photographic memory and many other things.

I am not telling you to completely abstain from sexual activity but you need to figure out the sweet spot how much you should engage in sexual activity. Yes, sex is good for your mental health. Balance is okay but there is no need to go to the extreme (complete sexual abstinence or overindulgence in sex), never overindulge in it. So that your motivation, drive, ambition does not get affected in the real world.

If you are the type of person who easily gets angry then sexual energy will amplify it more and if you are a calm person it will enhance more of it. So it's really important to work on your habits.

Many people are not able to get the maximum benefit of nofap because their habits are not allied with what they want to achieve. Nofap/ semen retention is just an accelerator. Sexual energy is very high voltage energy. It is not good or bad, but how you use that energy is the main thing. Even though if you fail in nofap which will happen for the majority – don't hold any negativity, guilt or shame, see what you can learn from it and start again.

Nofap will become a by-product of deep-focus work – It means when you will become so much focused on the work/ goal that you want to accomplish and let go of all your behaviours and thought patterns that restricting your growth. Example-: we all have a time in our life when we become so much focused on our work that we don't have any sexual thoughts, for a certain period of time, we were unconsciously following Nofap.

Benefit of nofap
1) Better and deep sleep
2) More confidence
3) More energized
4) Increase happiness
5) Heightened spirituality
6) Self-acceptance
7) Increase in muscle growth
8) Low stress and anxiety
9) Become more attractive to women
10) More focus and clarity
11) Deep voice
12) Become More charismatic
13) Boost the immune system
14) Increase life span
15) More self-control.
16) More creativity
17) More focus and concentration

When nofap/ semen retention is done in the wrong way then it will amplify your – frustration, anger, ego, causes anxiety, trouble in sleeping, lack of focus and concentration and set you in the hypersexual state - where you can't stop thinking of sex.

XXXI
New world of hyper-sexuality

In this chapter, we are going to talk about a question -: Where we are going with this society in terms of sexuality and the internet. If you are a regular internet user then you are aware of the fact that there are a large number of sexualized content that are made every day and which contain a large part of the internet because companies and creators are making a large profit from it.

Yes, the reality is that sex sells and a very large amount of people are present who wants to consume them. Companies and creators are capitalizing on the very strong human desire which is – sex. If you open any of your social media accounts from Instagram, Facebook you will find that most of the contents are mostly based on or related to sex.

You will find most videos on Facebook are based on something related to sex, you have also seen so many memes which are usually based on sex or sexualization of something. Creators are getting so many views and likes, as a result, they upload more of these contents because they want to grow their account as they are capitalizing from it from many sources – like affiliate marketing, sponsorship, building brands as they have audience/ people but it also rewires our whole generation to think about sex most of the time.

But the problem that arises from it is that whenever a person opens his phone/device then he/she is bombarded by sexualized content, as a result, sex becomes their thought pattern and that person thinks about it many times. We don't need to forget that desire for sex is one of the greatest desires of humans and due to this, it's also a very big source of distractions. Already social media were designed in a way that it could be more addictive and in addition to that when sexualized contents are also mostly present then it makes it more addictive. As a result of most people compulsively uses their social media. The reason why it is not good for us is that -: it changes our idea of sexuality – people start thinking that everything is related to sex, they might start objectification of people etc. Example -: While seeing a banana you may think about the penis, this happens because you have already seen so many contents where banana is sexualized. You might feel weird and uncomfortable in this chapter but there is an actual need to talk openly about it without any shame because that is happening in our society. No one has yet talked about it, so I am doing it so that you can be related to your life. Another reason why it's dangerous to consume these hyper-sexualized contents is that it imbalances your brain chemicals. Whenever you see this content your brain releases a high amount of chemical dopamine(feel-good hormones) so much, as a result, it becomes very hard for you to come out of it. But the main thing is that dopamine plays a major role in human motivation to act, and these sexualized contents drain your dopamine as a result you will be less motivated to take action in real life and towards your goals.

You have seen so many people especially –Teenagers and young adults that they are not feeling motivated towards their goals in life. And they have a problem with motivation, as they had already used their phone/ devices so much that it had drained the dopamine, so how can you expect to be driven and motivated. It's good advice to use your phone less in starting of the day so that you have more time for your goals and you will be less distracted.

Another thing is that this sexualized content usually acts as a trigger that directs you towards porn and this creates a loop of the addictive cycle. In the last two decades, the internet has come into our country and we need to consider the fact that it is very young. The majority of users are also young in it. It had never happened in history before that we had been opened to sexuality before. The amount of porn and sex content created and consumed in the last two decades had never happened before. We have never seen someone getting fame, great monetary value and even become millionaire by just selling sex in either inactive or passive ways. It has never happened before where people are establishing their careers and creating a great amount of wealth based on their beauty, hotness and sexiness. Instagram models are becoming famous with reels and by making tik-tok videos are all new concepts. People are confused that about what limit things are acceptable and unacceptable or cool from a sex point of view.

The majority of the creators of sexualized content in social media platforms belong to the age groups of 18-25 and these young people are seeing that they can easily make great fame, monetary value, attention and validation, love attention easily without putting much effort, so they get attracted to it. As they are young people they usually lack long term thinking and the future consequences. These people never think that after 20-30 years how they will going to feel about the work they had done whether they feel good or regretful. We had been entering into a new world of hyper-sexualization. We are surrounded by sex-sex sex as we are living in the internet era where sex is easily available, porn is present, there is live sex and live access to a person which had never had to happen before in history.

This does not mean that all things should be stopped and banned or we should stop using the internet. But the actual question is where we are going with sexuality and the internet. As the Internet is so young we do not have any data and researches which can tell about the impact of living in a hyper-sexualized society, its impact on us psychologically, socially and behavioural etc. A large number of young people are seeing this as an opportunity to capitalize on their beauty, sexiness/ hotness, so there is great competition to look sexier than others. As we are growing in the social media age, the majority of people are so much insecure about their bodies and not happy with their life because whenever these people open their Instagram they see – sexy, beautiful faces, people looking so much happy.

The majority of young people (18-25) are not able to think rationally that people in social media are selling them insecurities. Photos were highly edited/ filtered and taken with certain angles to appear sexy, vacation vlogs videos were well planned before and how can you judge someone vacations with 5 minutes clip. But because people are young and do not have an experience of reality, they accept the fact that whatever they are seeing on social media is the real thing.

The harsh reality is that no one care about your dreams and goals except you and your parents, if you are lucky you might have one-two more person in your life. Even your parents after some time will be comfortable when you get into a stable career. Only you will regret in life the things that you won't be able to achieve. So if you are someone who usually consumes these sexualized contents – porn, reels, photos etc regularly and wastes a lot of time in it then you need to come out of it. To achieve something in the real world, you need to first come out of the consumer mindset to the achiever mindset.

We are living in a capitalistic world, companies – wants profit, but if you are the one who is stuck in compulsively consuming(social media, Netflix, YouTube etc)you will never going to be an achiever because we have limited time and energy.

And to be in an achiever mindset, you need to make sacrifices to a certain extent, you need to be selective of what contents you give access to your brain so that it is helpful in the journey of your dreams and also help you to develop and grow as a person. You need to be dedicated to your goals and dedication as it does not come alone, it comes with focus and sacrifices. You need to first stop doing mental masturbation(thinking about sex without physically being involved in masturbation/sex or anything that stimulate your mind which distracts and imbalance your dopamine) from sexualised content as social media distracts you to be an achiever. I am not telling you to completely cut off from social media but I am telling you to set a limit, based on your goals and at what level you want to achieve, choose your level of sacrifice. The downside of growing hyper-sexualized is it rewires the whole generation to be obsessed and compulsively think about sex-sex sex most of the time which is quite a dangerous thing. What consumes your will mind rewires your mindset and behaviour which further dictates your actions.

Another important topic we are going to discuss is about -only fans and things similar to only fans. If you are not aware of what only-fans is then let me tell you that it's a platform where you can get paid by the consumers for selling them your content. It usually contains, workout videos, poetry, eBooks, food recipes, music. But this platform is mostly famous for X-rated content because the majority of creators are selling sex in some way. People are selling nude photos, strips and sex clips in it. Who is selling sex content? The answer is Instagram models, pornstars, YouTubers, influencers and common people as it is open for all. There might be chance that the person living in your city are using it. The majority of creators are women and most of the consumers are men. Yes, there is a vast population of men exists who wants and likes to see women online. Now we are dividing the only fans into two parts- first are creators and second are consumers.

Why there is the existence of creators who are selling sex? Why they are doing this? The answers is that they are making good money from it, women are getting attention and appreciation for their body which had never happened before.

But money is the major motivation for creators. Some models made millions of dollars within one week by using this platform.

Another question is why there is a large number of consumers on onlyfans even when free porn are available?

This is because it had never happened before in the entire history that you can have access to the nude/ sex content of someone you like. People not only from the adult world but from the real world sell their sexual content. When you open the only fans website, firstly you can only see the profile and some free content uploaded by the creator, just like other social media but the interesting thing is that it also provides creators to have private content(sex contents) that they want to sell (photos, videos). It never happened in the entire history that- first you find someone attractive (you may have a crush on then) and also have the opportunity to watch them naked just by paying money for that.

Another thing that separates it from porn is that in only fans people can feel connected more as creators and users can hold a conversation with each other or text each other. No matter how boring your text is creators will reply to them and also act interested in your life by asking you a question, remembering your birthday etc so that you feel connected to them. But in porn people do not feel the connection.

People use porn for arousal and fantasy, deep inside people are knowing that the sexy person they are watching on the screen does not know them, nor they are ever going to meet them or get the opportunity to hold a conversation with them, but in only fans, there is mutual interaction as they reply to messages and do this to make you feel connected, as a result, people get driven to put more money into it. As a result, people are choosing only fans over porn. I am not saying that the majority of men on this planet is using only fans but recent data tell us that there are 120 million viewers on it which are growing every day. This platform and others similar to it are capitalizing on how much somebody (usually a man) can pay for seeing someone (usually women) naked and also giving them a chance to form connections.

But another question arises – what is the actual problem people are facing which drives them to these websites. The answer is loneliness and rejection. Lonely fans of only fans. If you analyse the users you will find that majority of users are either lonely or rejected and also socially awkward. You will find that users had been rejected by women in their past, or they had never got into meaningful relationships, a huge portion of people don't have any friends with whom they can hang out, hold conversations and have fun. Even creators are lonely people because most men doesn't want to be in relationship with someone who strips clothes in only fans. But why people don't go out and form a real-life relationship, it's because forming a relationship takes effort and time, also there might be a chance of getting rejected. But connecting in the digital world does not require much effort and in a website like only fans you just need money to form it. There is no fear as there is no rejection, no matter how much boring, socially rejected you are, creators will hold a conversation with you and there is no fear of rejection in it. Even if you are not interested in a specific creator then you can easily switch to another creator.

What is the long-term impact on users and creators from these websites?

First, we will talk about creators-: usually young people mostly girls get into it for money, attention, love, validation without thinking about the long term consequences of it. They might be a chance that some people are seeing it as a career option and might see themselves as a business person because it's easy to sell sex compared to doing other work, also there is a large market for it. These people do not think in the long-term term how would their life look in the future – because their nude content will always be present on the internet. These people don't ask themselves that how it is going to affect my meaningful relationship in future, how their children see them for this kind of act – maybe they will hate you for this activity, maybe your parents also hates you and doesn't want to see you, maybe your neighbour sees you like a slut and try to bullies you, there might be a chance that one of your users find you in real life and try to kill or molest you etc. The reality is that you don't know the future consequence of what will going to happen. By doing this, creators are also contributing to the objectification of women by portraying them as sex objects just for the sake of money.

In addition to that, there is no data available on how these activity going to change your behaviour, affect your mental health, affect your social life etc. Second when we talk about users then there are so many adverse effects on them. First, it will affect your relationship, maybe you will never be able to get into a meaningful relationship until you come out of it and another point is that it rewiring your whole brain and changing it to see women as sex objects which will affect your relationship with women in your life in a bad way.

Over time more numbers add to your age you will find that you are left alone not having anyone talk to you and live with you because this loop is quite dangerous. You will end up being alone whole life, this website gives you the pseudo feeling that you have people with whom you can talk without any effort just in return for money, so you will not take action towards forming a relationship in the real world. It kills the chance of forming a deep meaningful relationship. It will effects your mental health badly and also decline your happiness index over the period.

The advice is simple to focus on forming real-life connections, if you are a socially awkward or introverted personality then try to learn social skills by interacting with more and more people.

Go out and make new friends, join groups according to your interest so that you can find more people of the example of the same interest – singing club, martial arts, gym etc. You need to come out of your comfort zone because things will not come if you are sitting on your sofa with your phone most of the time, you need to take action. In future, there will be digital girlfriends and friends who will capitalize on lonely people but it can never replace the real-life connection with people. Real-life connection is a necessity for sustaining good mental health and happiness.

The problem with young people in our country is that they are obsessed with sex and social media in some way, as a result, there is a very less amount of young people who are having an innovative and creative mind, fewer numbers of good players and young scientists etc. The reality is that no one is coming to take responsibility for your life. In order to deal with sex, sex content, social media etc you need to make your own set of rules to deal with them.

The main aim of this chapter was to make you aware of a hyper-sexualized society, its impact on our mindset, perception, behaviour and mental health.

XXXII
Fighting the rape culture

Rape culture is a term to describe a culture in which rape and sexual violence are common. Majority of sexual assault are done by someone who was close family relative, family members, friends and neighbours. According to national crime bureau data, 93% of rape in India is perpetrated by someone known to the victims. Eight out of ten rapes are committed by someone known to the victim. There are huge numbers of rape cases present which never got reported, just because the victim is blamed, shamed, people question character etc.

When the case of rape come to light then everyone starts becoming obsessed with fighting against it, does protest and candle March, which is a good thing but after few days everything goes to normal and this obsession comes again after a flash of the new rape case.

The problem is no one addressing the actual root problem and asking questions like why is rape happening so much?

According to 2018, Thomson Reuters Foundation reported India is the most dangerous place in the world for woman.

What is the actual cause of rape -:

1) Mind-set and attitude-: There are so many people in our country who believe that girls are also responsible for rape. These people are of different ages, different professions and educated peoples are also presenting it. Some believe that it is a part of society and will always go on. Many people compare clapping with rape and say clapping can't be done with one hand and say rape is consensual. In our society, people have so many negative beliefs that blame the victim and question her character.

They give reasons for rape like - walking in the street at night, wearing small and tight clothes, women using phones etc. Are women clad in sarees and burqas not raped? There are instances where men had been found doing sexual abuse to animals.

Should we dress animals too? Rapists allege that women are doing heavy makeup especially lipstick to seduce men, then how do you explain the rape of infants, old age women, women suffering from the soundness of mind and women in a comma. People rape their daughters, sisters and sometimes even mothers. The reason for this extreme depravity is an obsession with sex. There is a report of necrophilia(having sex with a dead body) in our country. Sexuality is so much suppressed in our country which led to obsession over it, men are not trained to "how to handle their sexual desire", just because of ignorance and watching sex as taboo.

Many believe that Panchayati law was good as it punishes both boy and girl but the state law gives leeway to the girl and only boy get trapped into it. They believe that the marriage of rapists with victims is the solution. We are living in a patriarchal society where men are put on a pedestal and his decision will be accepted and no or very little significance will be given to women in the major portion of our country which gives rise to a male-dominant society for a very long time, even we talk about equality between the gender but most of the people in our society does not want to accept it. They always want to suppress women and try to control them. There are so many families in India where women are not allowed to dress according to their choice, are not allowed to meet people, not allowed to do work.

In male dominant society, a women vagina become the site of her family honour and this honour is used as a cheat code to control women, in name of protecting that honour men can do anything, make decisions for her, control their life.

Our generation is the first where women start working, dress according to their choice, work till late at night, are going out for drinks and smokes etc. But the old patriarchal beliefs in people have not yet changed as a result there is resistance.

Men migrated to cities for work, they were aware of how women live in rural areas (conservative, take care of child and family, do not go for work, dress traditionally etc) then they see women in cities which were so different from their beliefs and what they have seen and and as a result, they start seeing women in cities as a slut, also there is a need of sex in them as they have come alone to earn money. As most of them were not educated and aware, porn shapes their wrong perception about women and sex which results in rape.

Solution-:

1) The solution is simple people need to accept the new generation. They should encourage women to live life the way they want to live, dress according to their choices, meet people etc. There should be total equality for both genders. Bad parenting and social environment also result in bad believe about women because discrimination is subconsciously taught in our society. So many parents in our country give more significance to boy child and less to girl child, this need to change and parents should treat both genders with equality in everything.

There is a vast part of society in our country were female are seen as a burden for the family. Their work is just to serve their family and to give babies to the family, they were prohibited from basic human rights and that's why female foeticides are happening in our country(especially in rural parts) this all are the result of the toxic male dominant society. Government and NGOs should take initiative to make people aware of the new culture in the rural areas.

I don't know why most people in our country try to see the existence of women in just two extreme perceptions either she is a goddess or she is slut. Why people don't see women as normal human beings just like you and I. We need to reduce the gap between both gender because many families do not allow to let their girls/boys even talk to the opposite gender of their ages, we send girls to girls college and boys to boys college, as a result, this form the beginning of their childhood and they start forming wrong assumptions, there is need to normalize and both genders are allowed to be friends.

Women are seen as eye candy and overly sexualised in many posters.

Indian cinema tries to normalize rape, many mainstream movies, web series, songs are contributing to the objectification of women.

There are item songs that portray that women are objects and they are just present on this planet for male sexual gratification. Consumption of these song subconsciously rewires males to see women as objects, most of the consumers are teenagers and it is shaping their minds. There is a need for improvement in the quality of Indian cinema and also elders should talk to their youngsters about how it is affecting their perceptions and mindsets to see the real world.

2) Lack of sex education-: We need to accept the fact that sex is seen as a taboo topic in our country and we try to avoid talking about it. Most men are sexually suppressed, they do not have the proper knowledge about sex. This high-speed internet and cheap data and smartphones are available to different sections of society (from rich to poor, urban to rural, illiterate to literate) and people are trying to learn about sex from porn. And we know what porn teaches us (violence, sex without consent, objectification of women, incest etc) as a result some people try to have sex with women without their consent which lead to rape because that is what porn teaches us.

Paedophile people (needed child to get orgasm) in our society are also present, which is also a reason for rape. These people become paedophiles because of excessive use of porn which rewires their brain to get turned on by girl children only. So there should be proper sex education in our society which is needed, people should have proper knowledge of menstruation, sexual intercourse, sex transmitting diseases, risks of pregnancy and masturbation. There are so many wrong belief made in rural area in our country about menstruation, girls are not allowed to enter the temple during this phase, this is just one example there are so many other negative beliefs associated with it. There is also a negative belief about masturbation that is widespread in our country all because of the lack of proper sex education.

Due to lack of sex education, there is so much sexual frustration in people, they do not know how to handle sexual desire because they have never trained for it.

It should be the role of parents to teach their child about the good touches and bad touches, they need to give sex education to their child according to his/ her age and they should be taught how they should react to bad touches and raising voice against it.

3) Lack of moral values -: Most child does not go through proper parenting, many of them were raised in a toxic environment where domestic violence was common. UNICEF report(2012) found that 53% of boys and 57% of girls between the age of 15 and 19 thought that men beating their wives was acceptable because of patriarchy . The way we look at women and how we treat them unequally, the child are not taught about the moral value like

• Respect people irrespective of their gender.

• There is no difference between men and women when it comes to equality.

• There should be always a boundary between relationships that should not be broken.

There are so many cases we read every day where father is raping his daughter, this happens when boundaries were broken and these rapist does not have any moral values.

Many parents in our country teach their children about – male dominance, rigid thoughts about caste and religion etc.

4)Lack of strict rules and fast judicial system -: In our country it is a Herculean task to even get complaints accepted and bringing justice for victims in India can be painfully slow. There are so many corrupt police and politician that make it more difficult. The case must be fast-tracked and there should be a fixed duration(3 to 6 months) in court for rape cases. There is a loophole in our judicial system which must be improved. Government should take the initiative to make amendments to the old systems.

5)Lack of brutal punishment -: There is no fear in people who are involved in rape just because there is not any brutal punishment for this crime.

Rapes are normalized and are not taken seriously in our society. When we study the psychology of rapists then we can find that they do not have any fear and they see rape as a normal and common thing in our society. They have so many negative emotions in them for women.

6)Alcohol and drugs -: Alcohol is something that makes your brain lose control over your senses and make you unconscious and unaware of the environment. When you consume alcohol, it will start expressing the thought which is suppressed and we know sex is one of that powerful desires.

Example-: Person who has suppressed anger for his neighbour will start abusing his neighbour after taking alcohol, in the same way sex suppressed person try to explore sex which results in rape. 60% of rape cases, on college campuses results from alcohol and drugs.

7) Abuse in childhood -: There is so much research that suggests bad parenting, a child raised in a toxic family environment where domestic violence was common, discrimination for any reason, getting less love, bullying etc led to the development of negative emotions which come out as sexual frustration which results to rape.

AUTHOR

Rahul Raj is a young emerging author who is, stepping into the world of psychology and philosophy with his book " The Modern Chanakya". He is among one of the youngest authors of India who is spreading philosophical ideas and insights. During his teenage, he observed that people around him were facing many problems which inspired him to help others so that they could avoid all unnecessary problems and suffering. He is a critical thinker and he's ace at it. He is presently a 2nd-year student, pursuing B.A. in Economics. He also loves to read books, paint and travel.

www.ingramcontent.com/pod-product-compliance
Lightning Source LLC
LaVergne TN
LVHW041919070526
838199LV00051BA/2668